NIGERIA'S INSURGENCY
AND
COUNTERTERRORISM
STRATEGIES

Psychology of Terrorism and Terrorism Emergency Preparedness

BOWIE SONNIE BOWEI, Ph.D

authorHOUSE®

AuthorHouse™ UK
1663 Liberty Drive
Bloomington, IN 47403 USA
www.authorhouse.co.uk
Phone: UK TFN: 0800 0148641 (Toll Free inside the UK)
*   UK Local: (02) 0369 56322 (+44 20 3695 6322 from outside the UK)*

Published by AuthorHouse 08/26/2022

ISBN: 978-1-7283-7494-9 (sc)
ISBN: 978-1-7283-7493-2 (e)

Print information available on the last page.

Contents

Foreword

It is indeed an honour for me to be called upon by Dr. Bowie Sonnie Bowei to write the foreword of his book titled "Nigeria's Insurgency and Counter Terrorism Strategies". I have read the book and have every reason to congratulate him. The book is well written and well researched on the genesis of terrorism in Nigeria.

Dr. Bowei outlined the causes of terrorism in Nigeria dating back to 1966 to the present day. He not only retraced the emergence of terrorism in Nigeria but also expanded on the wide dimension and emboldenment of the terrorists in each of the regions of Nigeria.

He mentioned that one of the principle causes of terrorism is religious bigotry sighting Maitatsine uprising that broke out in Kano in the 1970's and escalated to other parts of the North such as Borno, Yola and parts of Bauchi state as examples. He alluded to the fact that Maitatsine later became dormant only to metamorphose into what is today known as Boko Haram. The emergence of Boko Haram was encouraged by politicians who saw them as veritable tools in pursuit of their elections.

Dr. Bowei posits that the doctrine practiced by the religious sects has a lot to do with mentoring from clerics stemmed from the Wahabi theology. He also touched on the violent crisis in the Niger Delta region which was mainly caused by environmental degradation on the region by the operations of the Oil companies without adequate compensation for the destruction of the farm lands and fishing grounds. Similarly, the Indigenous People of Biafra (IPOB) came to prominence due to perceived injustice and marginalization meted to Igbos.

All in all, Bowei believes that some of the root causes of terrorism are fingered to religious bigotry, illiteracy, poverty and injustice.

He proffered solutions to these by bringing to the attention of the authorities concerned to take appropriate steps in order to ameliorate the problems. He dealt with many other factors of life bordering on social welfare, economic well-being, and destruction of infrastructure.

Finally, I wish to conclude that the book "Nigeria's Insurgency and Counter Terrorism Strategies" is a well written and researched document which should be read by government agencies, policy makers, security agencies and all students of history.

Major General (Dr.) Paul Tarfa, rtd, mni.

In memory of my best friend, mentor, and brother who shared ideas with me on developing methodologies to reduce threats of insecurity and insurgency in Nigeria and around the world. Our work will continue until our dreams of providing the sustainable solutions to security threats are achieved.

Air Commodore Emmanuel John Udenyi—
Rest in perfect peace.

1 | Insurgency and Strategies for Counter-Insurgency

Several attempts at defining *terrorism* have failed to produce a universally acceptable definition of the word. Although various definitions of *terrorism* exist, the common determinant is that terrorism is a premeditated, politically motivated act of violence carried out against noncombatant targets by militant groups or clandestine agents. This is not to say that there are no other targets, such as the military, and other casualties or motives for terrorism, such as ideology and social influences. The primary motive of a terrorist, however, is to garner the attention of a government, irrespective of the target.

Terrorism dates back to when humans first began using violence to achieve political ambitions and evolved through decades to become modern-day terrorism. Terrorism has been traced to the first century AD with Sicarri Zealots, a radical offshoot of the Zealots, which was active in Judaea province and tagged a terrorist group. While the early days of terrorist acts presented as actions against a state and were aimed at improving its systems, modern-day terrorism is characterized by violent attacks against particular political and/or religious orders. With increased sophistication in armament and cyber-technology, widespread fear is achieved routinely as governments grapple to stay one step ahead of the next crisis.

In Nigeria, terrorism has a variety of descriptions, depending on the motives and the religious and cultural backgrounds of its perpetrators. However, it has been officially defined as the following:

> An act intended or regarded as having been intended to force a government or an international organization to carry out or abstain from carrying out a certain act such as researching or developing a biological or chemical weapon without lawful authority, dissemination of information (be it true or false) aimed at causing panic, evoke violence or intimidation against government, a person or group of persons.[1]

In referencing this definition, one can safely say that terrorist acts have been occurring in Nigeria since 1966. This includes the Nigerian Civil War led by Odumegwu Ojukwu, whose plan was to force the Nigerian government to secede a part of the country to the Igbo tribe of eastern Nigeria.

Other such acts include military coups in Nigeria and various other violent attacks motivated by several factors which were termed justifiable or unjustifiable by different factions. Despite the ongoing discussions on the technical definitions surrounding terrorism, this book focuses on terrorism trends that align with the definition of terrorism locally and internationally and are conducted by groups such as Boko Haram, Movement for the Emancipation of the Niger Delta, and other terrorist sects during the early twenty-first century to the date of this publication.

This publication is result-orientated. It is my goal to eradicate the causes of terrorism and assist in the ultimate evolution of this issue, that must evolve from discussion to action. It suggests concrete strategies to counter terrorism, ultimately helping to reduce the impact of terrorist acts and possibly lead to the prevention of terrorism worldwide.

---

[1] Goitom, H. (2011). Nigeria: Senate, House Approve Anti-Terrorism Bill. Available at http://www.loc.gov/law/foreign-news/article/nigeria-senate-house-approve-anti-terrorism-bill/.

The Evolution of Terrorism in Nigeria

With Nigeria gaining independence from colonial rule in 1960, the history and dynamics of terrorism in Nigeria were traced through a sociopolitical lens. It should be noted that though terrorism began just as the nation turned six, the effects of terrorism at that time cannot be compared to what is being experienced in present-day Nigeria. The various eras of political presence in Nigeria had their peculiar contributions to the evolution and development of terrorism, beginning with the era that heralded the Nigerian Civil War in 1967.

Terrorism is an act that intended to instil fear in civilians. It is targeted at a government in an attempt to forcefully make it take decisions outside its democratic considerations and policies. This act can be carried out by an individual or group of individuals. By this description, the first act of terrorism in Nigeria was carried out by Nigerian soldiers of southeastern descent. These militants, known as the Biafra soldiers, were determined to forcefully break away from the Nigerian government and take control of their own territory. They had experienced years of tribal segregation and persecution of the Igbos for staging a military coup that strategically positioned the Igbo tribe to gain political power. Most of the masterminds in the coup were Igbos, and an Igbo head of state, General Aguiyi Ironsi, was installed.

The Biafra militants also had an economic motive. They wanted to control the nation's major financial resources from the lucrative oil production located in the Niger River Delta (Niger Delta) area of Nigeria.

Although the Biafra experience was classified as a civil war, it had all the trappings of terrorism and would be categorized as such today. This is evidenced by the attempt of the same Biafra people to force the Nigerian government to secede a portion of the country to form the Biafran nation. This act is being sponsored by the indigenous people of Biafra, who have been officially declared as terrorists by the government of Nigeria. Between 1967 and 1970, thousands of civilian lives were lost, and human rights violations—such as kidnapping, rape, and murder—occurred as a result of the Biafra uprising. Cases of indiscriminate assassinations, bombings, arson, human mutilation, and assaults were also recorded, with a death rate of approximately two million people.

Between 1970, when the Biafra war ended, and 1980, the nation experienced various minor sectional unrests which were easy for the government to address. A few units of the Nigerian military were usually dispatched to engage and contain threats of civil unrest at that time, and peace was always restored to the affected areas in a matter of days. Afterwards, the nature of terrorism in Nigeria transformed with the emergence of religiously motivated terrorist groups. Terrorist groups such as the Maitatsine sect, which was motivated by religious ideologies, evolved. They existed in the 1980s and caused havoc in northern Nigeria.

The Maitatsine sect was linked to Mohammed Marwa, an Islamic preacher born in 1927. Mohammed moved to settle in Kano at age eighteen, and he began his career as an Islamic scholar and preacher. Due to the extreme and bizarre nature of his sermons, and his endless fury against Western culture and its popularity in Nigeria, he was dubbed Maitatsine, meaning "the one who damns". His teachings avowed that the reading of books other than the Koran was sinful and an act of paganism. Maitatsine was disregarded by Nigeria's government until his sermons became increasingly disconcerting. The government waged a war against him beginning in the 1970s, leading to riots that got him and over four thousand of his followers killed in 1982.

After his death, his supporters began to rise up against the government and spread across northern Nigeria. The group, which by then had gained fame and was popularly known as the Maitatsine Movement, introduced violence in Bulumkutu, Gongola (now Adamawa State in north-eastern Nigeria), and Bauchi, killing over one thousand civilians. Although the group was cleared by constant military attacks, it is widely believed that the remnants of the Maitatsine Movement who were rooted in Gongola and Bauchi evolved into the radical extremist groups that emerged in 2002, when a group of Islamic clerics in Borno (a neighbouring state to Gongola) headed by Mohammed Yusuf evolved. Their thinking was deeply influenced by Wahhabi theology, which determinedly intended to turn Nigeria into a strictly Islamic state by imposing Sharia law in the entire country, including the Christian south. One of the groups that emerged from the fragments of Maitatsine, with similar motives, tactics, and even more devastating levels of impact on the government and its citizens, is the Boko Haram sect, a religious, ideologically motivated extremist group.

When the group was initially formed to influence political interests, Boko Haram was radical but not violent. Boko Haram gained financial and technical strength through politicians from Borno State, who armed and used youths as their political thugs to win elections. It is said that a former governor of Borno State, home of Boko Haram, recruited them for his political gains sometime around 2003.[2]

As a result of its atrocities, Boko Haram became more famous in 2006, when the Nigerian Department of State Security carried out multiple arrests, detaining and prosecuting its members. The killing of its leader resulted in reprisal attacks on the Nigeria Police Force headquarters, the United Nations House, and Saint Theresa Catholic Church, all in Abuja in 2011.[3] The terrorists' motives included religious extremism and resentment over the killing of their founder and other members, as well as the most acute and common rationale being poverty. Boko Haram adopted most of the tactics of the Niger Delta militants, including bombing locations with international interests, kidnapping for ransom, and exchange of detained members.

Between 2009 and 2020, Boko Haram launched several operations leading to mass violence within and around Africa's Lake Chad region, comprising of northern Nigeria, the south-eastern Niger, northern Cameroon, and western Chad. The group has killed an estimated 18,000 people, displaced millions, and caused a devastating humanitarian crisis in these regions. By killing 6,600 in 2014 alone, it was noted as the world's deadliest terror group.[4]

Boko Haram is mostly notorious for its violence against women and children. It was noted for this in April 2014, after kidnapping 276 girls from a secondary school in Chibok, Borno State, Nigeria. The group is known to use their female captives as sex and domestic slaves and as human

---

[2] Fabiyi, O., and Akasike, C. (2016). Sheriff Created Boko Haram. Punchonline. Available at https://punchng.com/sheriff-created-boko-haram-says-borno-ag/.

[3] Chinwokwu, E. C., and Michael, C. E. (2019). Militancy and Violence as a Catalyst to Kidnapping in Nigeria. *International Journal of Police Science and Management*. https//doi.org/10.1177/1461355719.

[4] Bukarti, A. B. (2020). The origins of Boko Haram and why it matters. Hudson Institute. Available at https://www.hudson.org/research/15608-the-origin-of-boko-haram-and-why-it-matters.

bombs. Their targets are mainly civilian locations, including markets, hospitals, Internally Displaced Persons (IDP) camps, and worship centres.

Boko Haram has recruited thousands of male Almajiri (young Islamic scholars) into its sect and established itself as a formidable force. Judging from 750 fatalities of security forces in 2019, Boko Haram has attained some form of strength to be reckoned with. Other than financial support from sponsors, Boko Haram is engaged in robbing and kidnapping to buy heavy weapons and sustain their logistic and operations requirements. They are also involved in piracy off the Nigerian coasts and smuggling of drugs. They are known to have in their arsenal heavy weapons used in launching attacks on military bases and police stations.

The Movement for the Emancipation of the Niger Delta is a socio-economically motivated militant group and the result of a combination of various militant groups and individuals consolidating to fight for the same cause within the Niger Delta region of Nigeria. This militant group, that has existed underground since 2002, launched its first official outing with a 2005 series of bomb blasts and the kidnapping of several Philippine and American oil workers in the Niger Delta region. Although greed had set in and some of the so-called militants were focused on making tremendous wealth for themselves and their families, the narrative behind the formation of militant groups was the neglect of the region by the federal government while usurping the wealth of the region, and also developing other regions (especially the north) of Nigeria with the wealth derived from the natural resources acquired from the Niger Delta.

Although serious armed conflicts existed in the Niger Delta region from as early as 1966 to the early 1990s, severe acts of terrorism in southern Nigeria, unfamiliar to counterterrorism agencies, came with their own tactics around 2003. The militants from the Niger Delta region were more sophisticated in their strategies and execution. They had territorial advantage over military personnel, who were not trained for combat in the Niger Delta terrain. In addition, they had a strong bargaining chip which they used against the government; they possessed the power of economic decapitation due to Nigeria's major reliance on the income generated through its oil pipelines. The majority of these facilities were installed in the Niger Delta region and distributed crude oil and petroleum products to other parts of the nation and the world. This implies that whenever pipelines are destroyed by terrorists in the Delta region, the economy of the country is threatened, and the GDP and the nation's economy are undercut by the terrorists.

While describing the evolution, special attention should be given to the general motives of terrorism in Nigeria which points clearly at poverty, social deprivation, neglect, greed, corruption, and nepotism to name a few contributing factors. Based on the various terrorist groups that have emerged in Nigeria, one or more of these factors are cited as the motivations for their emergence with the exception of Boko Haram. Boko Haram claims religious ideology as its primary motivation.

The evolution and motives of terrorism in Nigeria would be incomplete without mentioning that these lethal groups all began as local aids and supporters of various politicians in Nigeria and were either used to protect or do dirty jobs for their principals. Right after elections, the well-armed touts were abandoned by the politicians and left with few choices. The obvious choice for survival was to use their weapons to make a living. In Nigeria, especially in the Niger Delta region, terrorism is a viable business venture. Many terrorists who have headed groups such as Niger Delta Volunteer Force, Movement for the Emancipation of the Niger Delta, and Niger Delta Avengers have used the proceeds from kidnapping and negotiations from the government and oil companies to buy schools, homes, private jets, and hotels abroad. Thus, a new motive and a new form of terrorism may be classified as "incentivized comfort terrorism". Although the government has made efforts in mitigating the effects of and in combating terrorism, the artificial challenges the government has in combating terrorism in Nigeria appears to be a case of the oppressed feeding the oppressor and requires good governance as the solution to terrorism in Nigeria. Also, true federalism, meaningful dialogue, youth empowerment, and avoidance of corruption will suppress the development of terrorism in Nigeria. When this profound observation is broken down, it is possible to find the solutions which can put an end to terrorism.

Modern Terrorism in Nigeria

Militant groups gained strength through various tactics such as kidnapping expatriates and oil workers for ransom, and launching attacks on oil facilities, forcing the government to negotiate with them.[5] Some of these negotiations involved cash for arms, which conned the government and strengthened the terrorists' arsenal because their old arms were sold to the government and the profits used to acquire more sophisticated weapons. These terrorists also negotiated for the allocation of huge contracts between the government and its leaders. The Niger Delta Amnesty program, that granted state pardons to all terrorists from that region, also ensured that billions of dollars were allocated to them and their friends and families as monthly stipends. Vocational training was also negotiated and achieved some success. Building on these successes and making firm commitments to the abstention from repeating failed approaches are the cornerstones of eradicating terrorism.

With the strategy of negotiation once believed to be the sole solution to the problem, the Nigerian government yielded to terrorists' demands and were then plagued by further threats from these groups. Mismanagement of the resources assigned for the project, lack of professional engagement, and corruption on the part of the handlers were widespread and led to the reckless waste of over $40 billion on unprofitable training programs. More than 80 per cent of the trained terrorists were introduced to vocations that had no financial viability, while others were apportioned monthly stipends for merely sitting at home.[6] This flawed strategy, aimed at ending terrorism in the Niger Delta, only encouraged terrorists from the region to keep threatening the government.

Other militant groups in that region consisting of natives began to spring up. The natives felt entitled to the governments' gestures and

---

[5] International Criminal Court. (2013). Situation in Nigeria Article 5 Report. Available at https://www.icc-cpi.int/iccdocs/PIDS/docs/SAS%20-%20NGA%20 -%20Public%20version%20Article%205%20Report%20-%2005%20August%20 2013.PDF.

[6] Wodu, N. (2014). A Look into the Niger Delta Amnesty Program—Success or Failure? Niger Delta Information Hub. Retrieved from https://ndlink. org/2014/01/28/a-look- into-the-niger delta-amnesty-program-success-or-failure/.

wanted to enjoy personal benefits. These natives should no longer be merely classified as terrorists but perhaps more aptly described as terrorists of opportunity.

Prior to the formation of the Niger Delta militant groups, Boko Haram registered scanty and barely noticeable attacks on facilities and civilians. However, when terrorists from the Niger Delta were captured by the Department of State Security and locked in the same cells with captured Boko Haram members, the northern terrorists gained access to knowledge of more sophisticated tactics from these militants from the Niger Delta, who were generous with disseminating information and ideas to their cellmates. The Department of State Security assumed that putting members of different terrorist groups together would break them because of their cultural and religious differences, but the terrorists saw it as an opportunity to share ideas, experiences, and tactics. As a result, Boko Haram began to duplicate the tactics of the Niger Delta terrorists. Explosives were introduced in the north along with kidnapping, both of which had not been part of Boko Haram's previous tactics for negotiations with the Nigerian government.

Over the years, and especially between 2001 and 2016, Nigeria suffered major casualties from Boko Haram attacks. Within this period, as many as 18,914 lives—both civilians and military—were lost, children were kidnapped and deprived of education and parental care, and communities were destroyed. These barrage of terrorist acts have left the nation with colossal social devastation and economic damage. In addition, the military tactics used to disengage terrorists, which basically are hunting down, locking up, and killing insurgents, are the same combat engagement strategies that infuriate terrorists and result in reprisal attacks on lives and property, costing the nation billions of dollars.

One major problem counterterrorist agencies in Nigeria are faced with is the inability to fully dissect the tactics of terrorists and agree on the best ways to approach them. As noted by one of Nigeria's presidents, Muhammadu Buhari, it is necessary that counterterrorist agencies strengthen their strategies and develop new ones to beat the terrorists at their game.[7] Sustainable solutions are required to combat terrorism. One

---

[7] *Punch News* (2017). Develop new strategies to fight Boko Haram. Retrieved from http://punchng.com/develop-new-strategies-to-fight-boko-haram-buhari-tells-army/.

such approach requires a collective commitment to conflict resolution; the civilian community and government must work together to confront terrorism. Communication is the key. By disseminating reliable information leading to the capture of prominent terrorists and providing intelligence that may thwart the successful operations of terrorists, a nationwide call to action is essential. That being said, strong incentives are needed to motivate citizens to risk their personal safety to achieve positive results.

The Nigerian state struggles with the ability to fully integrate active civilian participation in counterterrorism partly because all agents fighting against terrorism in Nigeria appear suspect and often viewed as enablers of terrorist activities. Reporters have often cited cases of individuals charged with the oversight of these issues who have succumbed to nefarious relations with terrorists. Examples of these are the cases of military officers and political office holders who have been caught in this practice and sanctioned by relevant authorities. One clear case is that of ten Nigerian army generals and five other officers found guilty of providing arms and information to Boko Haram, thereby sabotaging the operations of the army's engagements against insurgents in 2014.[8]

Antiterrorism agencies, including vigilante groups, assume that any civilian who may have useful information on terrorists may also be a terrorist. This has, in most cases, led to precarious consequences for civilians who have tried to help by providing intelligence reports to the military. Nonetheless, understanding the tactics of terrorists is a major tool towards defeating them. Nigerian counterterrorists lack this skill and need education and training in creative ways to tackle this problem through various result-oriented strategies rather than mere combat engagements.

The growing presence of terrorists in Nigeria has affected the educational development of youths in northern and southern Nigeria because the youth are recruited, indoctrinated by terrorist sects, or kidnapped and kept hostage for part of their lives. Social and economic development have been hampered by these recurring episodes as a huge

---

[8] Wiener-Bronner, D. (2014). Nigerian military officers court-martialed for giving Boko Haram weapons. *The Atlantic*. Available at https//www.the atlantic. com/international/archive/2014/06/Nigerian-generals-arrested-for-giving-boko-haram-weapons/372052/.

portion of the nation's wealth is directed towards fighting terrorism rather than funding and advance socioeconomic interests and progression.

As a result, the rate of poverty has increased. Most vulnerable Nigerian youths, therefore, have no option but to join terrorist groups as a means of livelihood to gain some form of power and benefits, including meals, sex with female victims, and stipends. These so-called necessities and benefits were far out of reach for them before their involvement with the terrorist groups, and this motivates them to join. The negative impacts of these terrorist groups in Nigeria have been globally noted and maintain steady growth. Nigeria ranks third-highest in terms of the worst impact of terrorism, behind only Iraq and Afghanistan.[9]

Various agencies in Nigeria and its neighbouring countries have been established to fight terrorism but without success. This is evident by the steady increase in casualties that include the military and other security agencies, tourists, expatriates, and first responders, despite the heavy presence of counterterrorist agencies. With the increasing rate of terrorism in Nigeria and its imminent spread across the African continent, the development of operative approaches to prevent and eliminate terrorism is important. Doing so will sustain a peaceful nation through planning and implementation of effective counterterrorism strategies and introduce positive social change among the nation's youth, while ensuring peace and stability.

Terrorism has been a part of the sociopolitical scenario in the global society. Since Nigeria's independence in 1960, millions of civilians have been killed for various reasons bordering around agitation against the Nigerian government for exclusion of their regions from socioeconomic benefits. As I examine the impact of increased exclusionist political attitudes towards minority groups and how a revisit of these policies may serve as a counterterrorist strategy to remedy the growing rate of terrorism in Nigeria, it is important that the attention of stakeholders is drawn to this critical factor.

Ethnic exclusionism reveals various forms of social phenomena which indicate that the majority in a particular society wishes to exclude minorities.

---

[9] Global Terrorists Index. (2017). Measuring and Understanding the Impact of Terrorism. Available at https://reliefweb.int/sites/reliefweb.int/files/resources/Global%20Terrorism%20Index%202017%20%284%29.pdf.

While some researchers argue that exclusionist political attitudes are common and destructive examples of non-democratic practices, Nigeria experiences ethnic exclusionism in all forms of ruling atmospheres, be they non-democratic or democratic. This is largely responsible for the economic deprivation in some ethnic regions, resulting in their aggressive approaches to terrorism as the only way out of a depressed situation. Exclusionism also affects the government structure in Nigeria as a number of government agencies or organizations are left to suffer, depending on the relationship between the legislative and executive arms of government. While the military depends on the legislative and executive arms of government to approve policies and funding for the fight against terrorism, corruption and politics within the system act as some of the reasons hindering the success in the fight against terrorism in Nigeria.

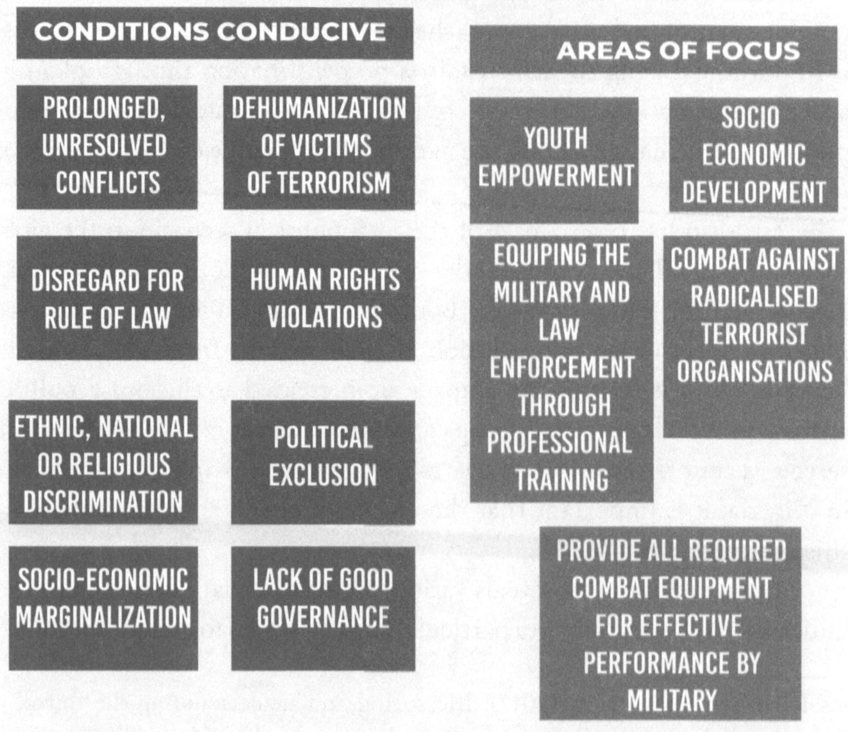

Application of Theories

Critical theory offers a descriptive and normative foundation for social inquiry and is designed to decrease domination and increase freedom in all forms.[10] In this case, it is applied through critiquing and analysing the social issues responsible for the domination of tribes that have emerged as terrorists using inhumanity as a justification for their actions. It is also concerned with critiquing and changing society in its entirety. Critical theory was developed in response to conventional approaches to uncover the ideological, conceptual, and institutional foundations of terrorism. It is used to critique dominant conventional approaches that link terrorism with technical capitalism, and claims that violent activities used by the state in a case of state terrorism against its own citizens have been ignored by traditional terrorism scholars. It is aimed at digging into social lives to reveal the assumptions that keep people from true and complete understanding of how the world works. Critical theory emerged from the Marxist tradition and was advanced by a group of sociologists at the University of Frankfurt in Germany, referred to as the Frankfurt School.[11]

Nigerians are being subjugated by terrorism and yearn for freedom. This may be achieved through the application of critical theory in seeking to liberate its citizens from the grip of terrorism by stressing the reflective assessment and critique of society and culture through the application of knowledge. Various geographic areas in Nigeria—such as the eastern, southern, and middle belt regions—have experienced years of government domination. They have attempted to gain their freedom in several unconstitutional ways. This has led to diverse forms of agitation beginning with what resulted in the Nigerian Civil War in 1967.

The next form of agitation resulting from the same causes gave rise to the formation of various militant sects in the Niger Delta, which gradually but steadily developed into terrorist groups. Through this perspective,

---

[10] Hoffman, M. (1989). Critical theory of the inter-paradigm debate. *The Study of International Relations*. Available at http://scholar.google.com/scholar?hl=en&as_sdt=0%2C5&as_vis=1&q=descriptive+and+normative+foundation+of+critical+theory&btnG=#d=gs_qabs&u=%23p%3Dpz9iARKU_aoJ.
[11] Crossman, A. (2019). *Understanding Critical Theory*. ThoghtCo. Retrieved from https://www.thoughtco.com/critical-theory-3026623.

counterterrorists must take critical steps to review issues and work out modalities to free citizens from oppression and to create the freedom that will enable peace, as well as economic and social development, rather than engage in combat operations as the only available strategy to combat insurgency.

Various theories ascertain that the major cause of terrorism in Nigeria is poverty. Because some corrupt government officials and leaders of counterterrorist agencies have been involved in siphoning wealth while their subjects languish in poverty, this situation can also be seen as domination of the less privileged. While terrorists are equipped with modern technology, efficient training, high morale, and effective tools to defeat the military, counterterrorists are ill-equipped and caged in a series of issues that discourage and hinder their success.

The Metele terrorist attack in Nigeria in October 2018 is one example of military forces experiencing lack of adequate equipment to engage terrorists, as well as lack of good logistic and moral support. A better-equipped and motivated terrorist group penetrated the fortress of the Nigerian military with ease and overran them, causing a devastating effect on the military and nation as a whole. Hundreds of soldiers were killed due to insider involvement and the lack of effective defence strategies, logistic support, and fighting tools.[12]

Looking critically at the causes of terrorism in Nigeria and the strategies applied in countering insurgency, state terrorism, that encompasses violent action against citizens, neglect, domination, and deprivation, has been a leading cause of terrorism in Nigeria. These must be addressed as one of the strategies to combat terrorism. In consideration of the fact that "a theory is critical to the extent that it seeks human emancipation from oppression, acts as a liberating influence, and works to create a world which satisfies the needs and powers of human beings",[13] counterterrorism strategies applied in Nigeria must absorb these considerations in seeking solutions to insurgency.

---

[12] Peterside, Z. B. (2014). The military and internal security challenges in Nigeria: Challenges and prospects. *Mediterranean Journal of Social Sciences* 5(27). DOI: 10.5901/mjss.2014.v5n27p1301.

[13] Horkheimer, M. (2009). Critical theory. *Stanford Encyclopedia of Philosophy*. Retrieved from https://plato.stanford.edu/entries/horkheimer/.

Another concept, resource dependency theory, highlights the relationship between organizations and the resources they need to operate. These resources may include training, developing a workforce, infrastructure, and funding. If an institution controls most of a resource, then another will become dependent on it to operate, creating a symbiotic relationship. In Nigeria, the security agencies depend on the government, with intermittent interjections from the legislative arm, to operate, creating the risk of external control resulting in uncertainty. External control, such as funding or policies, in Nigeria is enforced by the government and can have a negative effect on counterterrorist operations.

For organizations or countries to resist or overcome hardships, there must be a considerable amount of exchange in terms of human and capital resources. Its relevance will be found in highlighting the importance of resources and empowerment through education and training in the fight against terrorism. As resource dependency theory highlights, the resources they need to operate may include training, a workforce, infrastructure, and funding.

Resource dependence is not applied to only policies and finances. And it does not affect terrorism only in ways where finance or policies by those in power must be exchanged for effective engagement of terrorists. Natural resource dependency also has a way of promoting agitation or motivating the adoption of peace through detailed execution of well-structured strategies. The role that wealth or hoarding of natural resources plays as either a financing mechanism or promotional tool for agitation by state and non-state actors can be determined by a government as a strategy for peace and reconciliation. Regarding motivational elements of civil conflict, abundance of natural resources may spur would-be rebels to gain political control of territory from which they can extract resource wealth for economic dependence on the trading of commodities. Since economic motivations trump grievance motivations in most cases of terrorism in Nigeria, as proven by the poorly structured Niger Delta Amnesty Program (which was set up by the federal government of Nigeria to empower former militants of the Niger Delta as a means to stall agitation), practical strategies can be mapped out to use natural resources as tools for peace and stability in Nigeria.

The Importance of Knowledge

It is important to focus on the positive outcome expected to evolve from studying the security situation in Nigeria and introduce positive social change by eliminating terrorism. This can be achieved by ensuring that all the elements that motivate terrorism are taken out of the society by developing strategies to approach counterterrorism in Nigeria and address the menace of Boko Haram, Niger Delta militants, and other terrorists. This book provides insight into the necessity of education and youth empowerment as means of positive engagement to discourage poverty-driven motives for becoming terrorists. It therefore should allow for programs that implement effective counterterrorism training in the military and other security institutions to be put in place while providing new policies that will ensure these strategies are brought to fruition. Although the addition of new strategies to existing ones used by the military is vital in winning the fight against terrorism in Nigeria, strategies that focus on military operations that encourage only the use of force must be discouraged. As terrorists continue to develop new tactics to defeat opposition and achieve their aims, the implementation and continuous development of viable counterterrorism strategies is essential.

The author intends to advance the scope of counterterrorism strategy building and improve the development of defined roles and responsibilities for engagement of stakeholders by providing the necessary tools required to enhance cooperation among all stakeholders and a better understanding of their roles and responsibilities in combating insurgency. Notwithstanding the efforts made towards curbing insurgency in Nigeria, the negative effects on communities, individuals, the economy, and the image of the country are spreading and gaining ground. Terrorism has a negative effect on those responsible for perpetrating the act and those affected by the act. Most affected by terrorism are the youths who ought to be in school. Some are inducted into terrorist groups while others are kidnapped and forced to carry out acts of terrorism. Knowledge and education provide a better society, so preventing young people from achieving this social necessity is a way of taking society backward. In Nigeria, thousands of young terrorists and students are kept away from school as a result of terrorism and its impact on the society.

Developing strategies that would ensure citizens regain their positions to enjoy these basic benefits would help in creating positive social change. Enabling young people to gain some form of economic empowerment and education will ensure that society improves. Awareness of community counterterrorism involvement will decrease the chances of regular devastating attacks on communities that prevent them from enjoying social benefits as a result of fear or physical damage. Knowledge would also reveal the importance of development and the roles education and training play in a society. This will ensure that the rate of government dependency decreases, and the citizenry becomes a productive part of creating social change in and around their communities.

Although various strategies have been applied towards the eradication of terrorism globally, it persists, and various new motives for acts of terrorism continue to develop. Likewise, as counterterrorist agencies develop new strategies to fight insurgency, terrorists also develop workable tactics to beat counterterrorists and ensure that their impact is felt globally and their demands met.

The overall issue with the inability to curb terrorism in Nigeria is more of an administrative problem, where technical and financial resources, as well as policies and their implementations, are either not sufficiently applied or are not put in proper sequence. This may be a result of stakeholders' other interests, such as diversion of funds assigned for the purpose of acquiring security equipment for their personal use; political differences among policymakers that result in delays in legislative decisions, causing grievous security implications; or lack of expertise and execution of counterterrorism strategies and applications.

To address terrorism effectively in Nigeria, all stakeholders need to understand the various roles they are to play. Citizens must understand and be educated on their roles; the military and other security agencies must also be educated on their roles and the importance of the roles of civilians in combating terrorism; policymakers and heads of security agencies must understand that working as a team towards achieving the same goal of eradicating terrorism in Nigeria is imperative. Bearing in mind that this book intends to develop understanding, educate all stakeholders, and advance the strategies applied in counterterrorism operations in Nigeria, the author has attempted to give account of the various motives of terrorists in Nigeria. The experience, strengths, and weaknesses of counterterrorist agencies; strategies that have been used and their limitations; the reasons for youth vulnerability in being enlisted in terrorist groups; social motivation of young terrorists against the motivation of counterterrorist personnel; and the importance and need for developing new and workable strategies have also been dicussed in detail.

The gap in the strategies used by counterterrorists in Nigeria may result from lack of proper training and understanding of the concept of terrorism and counterterrorism. One vital point in creating strategies is to critically understand the concept, bearing in mind the motives of terrorists, the underlying factors responsible for their choices to become terrorists, the benefits derived from their involvement, and their level of understanding and intelligence. Based on these, proper assessment of various strategies should be made with various considerations, and those that best apply may be used depending on issues such as religion, level of education, social exposure, and, of course, the fighting strength of the terrorists.

Causes and Consequences of Terrorism in Africa

In Africa, one of the major causes of terrorism has been identified as poverty. Though religious ideology has to an extent been said to be a cause of terrorism in Africa, the reason recruitment of militants by these religious terrorists appears to be easy is because those who are seen as vulnerable targets for recruitment are mostly youths and teenagers engulfed in poverty. This has been attributed largely to the theory of deprivation resulting from corrupt or incompetent leaders and mismanagement of resources, and it applies to most countries in Africa.[14] Although relative deprivation theory has been the main explanation for terrorism in Nigeria and Africa as a whole, this theory may no longer be valid as the primary reason for violence, though it may function as a weighty contributing factor in a few social circumstances, such as the cases of outright and intentional

---

[14] Elu, J., and Gregory, P. (2015). *The Oxford Handbook of Africa and Economics: Economics and Finance, Economic Development, International Economics. Volume 1: Context and Concepts.* Edited by Célestin Monga and Justin Yifu Lin. DOI: 10.1093/oxfordhb/9780199687114.013.16.

government neglect of certain regions within the country while others are being developed.

In sub-Saharan Africa between 1974 and 2004, over 4,993 terrorism incidences occurred, with 261 terrorist groups claiming responsibility for them. Statistics reveal that the number of Muslims in Africa far exceed the number in the Middle East, indicating that this may be a reason for a higher level of radical Islamist presence and actions in Africa. African countries that are mostly hit by terrorism are governed by democracy and are those prone to terrorism. Those under military rule may have little terrorist impact. This may most likely be as a result of the heavy presence of the military and the ruthless measures taken against enemies of the state in such countries.[15]

Economic and political factors were also identified as being responsible for terrorism in Africa. In line with the poor and unbearable economic situation in Nigeria and the pressing need for survival, especially by youths who are physically active, it can be said that one of the major causes and motivations for terrorism in Nigeria is poverty. This is referenced by the Niger Delta Amnesty initiative, that was put in place by the Nigerian government to provide economic relief for terrorists from the Niger Delta area as a strategy for peace in the region. To a large extent, the strategy worked while the supply of financial resources and social benefits were available. With the change of government to the Buhari administration, the release of funds to the Niger Delta militants was initially stopped, resulting in the emergence of new terrorist groups, such as the Niger Delta Avengers. Funds and benefits were reintroduced to the terrorists, and terrorism in the Delta ceased to exist.

As this book focuses on terrorism in Nigeria, it is important to lay emphasis on its causes and consequences in Nigeria, which include but are not limited to illiteracy, poverty, and social deprivation. The Niger Delta region hosts the nation's wealth and main source of revenue because all other revenue-generating tools had been grounded as a result of mismanagement and sole dependence on oil. Prior to the total dependence

---

[15] Elu, J., and Gregory, P. (2015). *The Oxford Handbook of Africa and Economics: Economics and Finance, Economic Development, International Economics. Volume 1: Context and Concepts.* Edited by Célestin Monga and Justin Yifu Lin. DOI: 10.1093/oxfordhb/9780199687114.013.16

on oil from the Niger Delta region as the nation's source of revenue, Nigeria generated income from agriculture and other natural resources, including iron ore, tin ore, limestone, coal, lead, zinc, columbine, marbles, bitumen, and tar sand.

Unfortunately, after the mismanagement of the nation's other natural resources and focusing on resources coming from one source (crude oil), it became impossible for the government to satisfy all the geopolitical regions of Nigeria, especially the Niger Delta region. In addition to the neglect of the Niger Delta region, the people of the Delta were further impoverished by foreign oil companies who polluted the environment, destroying their only sources of livelihood, fishing and farming.

As a result of poverty due to neglect and assault by the government and oil companies, youth of the Niger Delta resorted to unhealthy protests and subsequently, full-blown terrorism, or militancy, as they called it.

The north-east, where Boko Haram has its fortress, is quite different. Though the main motive is religiously inclined, recruitment and sustenance of militants would have been impossible if not for poverty. Generally, the north is known to have wealthy politicians and poor and uneducated citizens, most of them registered as Almajiri. The Almajiri are Islamic scholars and mostly minors. They grow up begging for alms and engage in any act that may assure them of their next meal. They have been identified as involved in all religious riots in the north and are always eager to participate in the opportunity to loot homes and shops of their victims as a means of survival. They form the foot soldiers of Boko Haram and other terrorist groups in northern Nigeria as the promoters of terrorism in this area take advantage of their vulnerability and desperation for survival.[16]

In summary, the consequences of terrorism in Nigeria, and Africa in general, considering the major underlying factors, are a deadly trend of citizens enrolling as terrorists and seeing terrorism as a trade or a viable business venture. This appears to be the fastest way out of poverty and social deprivation as social benefits which were far reaching are achieved in the camps. Insurgents are paid, fed, and have female kidnapped victims at their disposal for sex. This may mean that as long as the economic

---

[16] Dahiru, M. (2018). Almajiri as a Consequence of Boko Haram. Blueprint news. Retrieved from https://www.blueprint.ng/almajiri-consequence-boko-haram-majeed-dahiru/.

and social situation does not improve and positively affect these actors, terrorism resulting from the three previously mentioned issues will persist and become irrepressible.

The Effect of Bad Governance

Nigeria's story of nepotism, neglect, and deprivation among its citizens started from the military regimes that governed the country, beginning with General Aguiyi Ironsi's reign as head of state between January and July 1966. This was the beginning of a tribal division in Nigeria as northern military officers overthrew the government headed by a south-easterner, presenting allegations of tribal segregation and neglect of the north and west of Nigeria (Lodge, 2018).

Nigeria has experienced series of military rules since independence. The reasons for the steady overthrow of governments were pegged on the fact that most of the selected military or democratically elected leaders were corrupt. Unfortunately, the military leaders who took power each time were known to have been more corrupt than those they accused. This means that Nigeria has had a continuous cycle of leaders and governments that are corrupt, and are all part of the reasons terrorist groups have formed across the country, following the theory that corruption gave rise to neglect and deprivation of citizens. This is not far from the truth as there would have been no agitation if the citizens were satisfied. Once a gap for expression of disatisfaction by citizens of a country is created, this may give rise to opposition groups that may turn violent when trying to defend themselves from attacks by authorities, and eventually evolve into terrorist groups.

In addition, the absence of developmental projects and social amenities led to poverty in the country and opened the avenue for politicians to make use of youths as touts. This led to youths experiencing the use of force in achieving demands and exposed them to power and greed. In a way to sustain their vices, ideology was used as the motive for their terrorist drive in the north. Boko Haram as a sect began to grow due to the appealing social benefits offered to members while recruiting them from the Almajiri pool. Other than poverty, cultural and religious practices in northern

Nigeria stand out as motivating factors for female enlistment into the Boko Haram sect.

Whereas male recruits may be forced into the group or lured through various enticements, most of the female recruits (other than those captured) willingly join the sect. This is a result of the culture in the north, which interferes with their rights to freedom. Early marriage, lack of education, and domestic violence are common among women and girls in the north. To escape from these forms of domestic and cultural slavery, women are voluntarily enlisted into terrorist sects to afford themselves the opportunities to negotiate restricted freedoms in a highly constrained environment. As women in northern Nigeria rely on religion for a space of relative independence, Boko Haram has clearly been seen by many women to provide such opportunities.

The Niger Delta Agitation

Agriculture was the main source of revenue in Nigeria prior to and immediately after independence in 1960, until after the first military coup in 1966. Then came the period of the oil boom between 1971 and 1979, when the international market increased its oil price. These two events brought a change in Nigerian politics and economy as the country experienced a change in its economic focus by dumping agriculture and concentrating its focus on oil exports. With the abolishing of regional federalism, marginalization, corruption, and neglect of certain areas of the country set in, and conflicts, especially in the Niger Delta region, began.[17]

The reason for marginalization of the Niger Delta region by the federal government was as a result of the aggression exhibited by the dwellers of the region against the government and other tribes in Nigeria. However, it is my opinion that aggressive agitation should not have been punished with deprivation of the benefits in a region, especially as that region produced the major source of income for the country. This, under

---

[17] Adetunberu, O., and Bello, A. O. (2018). Agitations in the Niger Delta region, oil politics and the clamours for restructuring in Nigeria. *International Journal of Peace and Conflict Studies* (IJPCS) 5(1). Available at http://www.rcmss.com/index.php/ijpcs;www.academix.ng.

normal circumstances, would cause an uprising, as seen by the formation of various militant groups and the negative effect it has on the nation's economy resulting from militant activities in the Niger Delta region.

Terrorism in the name of agitation began in the Niger Delta in 1966 with Jasper Isaac Adaka Boko, who was involved in the struggle for resource control resulting from the underdevelopment and neglect of the region by the federal government. Over the years, a series of groups were formed with the same motive to ensure that the region controls its resources. This motive was accompanied by various attacks on government by groups in the Delta. In most cases, civilians have been directly or indirectly affected by the operations of militants in ways like kidnapping and reprisal attacks on civilian communities by the Nigerian military.

Ken Saro-Wiwa led the Movement for the Survival of the Ogoni People in 1990 to revolt against the government over the same issues. Eight years after, in 1998, the Kaiama declaration by Ijaw youths from over five hundred communities opened the floodgates for revolution, and various terrorists groups have emerged since then.[18] The most significant of these groups, however, is the Movement for the Emancipation of the Niger Delta, whose impact was felt within Nigeria and the global community from 2003 to 2010. They ensured that the economy of the nation was crippled through constant attacks on oil pipelines, military formations, and foreign oil companies. Their major strategies were kidnapping for ransom to sustain the group, bombing of pipelines to adversely affect the nation's economy, and attacks on military formations to establish their authority and create fear. In this regard, the military and civilians, as well as the international community in Nigeria, were all affected.

The Role of Corruption and Other Challenges

The Nigerian military is said to be the strongest military in Africa as it has been battle tested on various peacekeeping missions. Congo, Sierra Leone, Liberia, and Sudan are a few beneficiaries of the Nigerian

---

[18] Ojo, M. O. (2015). Militia uprising in the Niger Delta and its implications for national security. *International Journal of Development and Sustainability* 4(9). Available at www.isdsnet.com/ijds.

military's support. The strength of the military, to some extent, is drawn from the level of morale they possess, which contributes to their success in times of war. The morale of a Nigerian soldier is weighed in most cases by logistical support in terms of the benefits that are given to him during and after the operation, how well he is taken care of on the battlefield, and the availability of ideal and efficient tools—weapons—required to give him an upper hand against his enemies.

To combat insurgency, a lot of resources are required. Boko Haram is well equipped with sophisticated weapons acquired from attacks on Nigerian military armories and the international black market.[19] It is therefore required that superior firepower must be acquired for the Nigerian military to ensure they match up with Boko Haram and other well-equipped terror goups. Unfortunately, when the engagement of terrorists began, rather than seeing the importance of winning the fight against terrorism, military authorities were more interested in using the opportunity to make a fortune for themselves. The biggest arms purchase scandal in Nigeria involved military authorities and top government officials, when two billion dollars were released for the purchase of weapons to fight terrorism in 2015.[20]

The reason for prolonged insurgency in Nigeria and the lack of effective machinery to engage terrorists is the result of the diversion of funds assigned for combating security challenges, the purchase of obsolete and poor-quality weapons, the formation of phony defense contracts, and the absence of logistical support for soldiers combating insurgency. As training and welfare of counterterrorist agencies is of paramount importance, it therefore means that with the provision of appropriate and effective weapons for the military, and without proper counterterrorism training and the required morale and logistic support, the military will not achieve its aim in defeating terrorists. While they have all they require to fight insurgency, the human resources to be used in fighting will be weak

---

[19] Campbell, J. (2014). *Nigeria's Boko Haram and Heavy Weapons.* Council on Foreign Relations. Retrieved from https://www.cfr.org/blog/nigerias-boko-haram-and-heavy-weapons.

[20] Perlo-Freeman, S. (2017). *Nigeria's Armsgate Scandal. A Compendium of Arms Trade Corruption.* World Peace Foundation. Available at https://sites.tufts.edu/corruptarmsdeals/nigerias-armsgate-scandal/.

and create a gap in the components that are necessary for achieving success in the fight against insurgency.

The Nigerian military, due to corrupt practices, shut its eyes to ethical conducts and weakened its forces by diverting funds meant for soldiers' welfare in addition to funds they diverted from weapons and equipment purchases. This allowed Boko Haram to seize the opportunity to overpower the military during many attacks. In fact, Boko Haram overran military formations, kidnapped wives and children of soldiers, and went with large catchments of arms and ammunition at various times. The effect of corruption by the military and its cohorts, especially as regards terrorism, is the trigger for the strengthening of Boko Haram and other terrorist groups in Nigeria and has caused colossal loss of lives and property of the military, civilian citizens, expatriates, and foreign aid workers.

Insurgency and National Security Challenges

In the same way Boko Haram gained strength in the north-east, the Movement for the Emancipation of the Niger Delta became formidable in the south through the inability of the Nigerian military to contain terrorism in the Delta region. Both sects have a common source fuelling their motive, poverty. Poverty has been the driving force and will continue to motivate Nigerian youths to engage in terrorism irrespective of their geopolitical origin until government and military authorities take decisive and strategic steps to end insurgency.

The tactics of Boko Haram and the Movement for the Emancipation of Niger Delta were a little different until the Department of State Security began to keep arrested members of both sects together between 2005 and 2010. The game changed afterwards, and it became evident that the modern techniques used by the Movement for the Emancipation of the Niger Delta in the south were replicated in the north. This made it more difficult for security agencies to contain Boko Haram as the military was overwhelmed by their new tactics which included the kidnapping of students and expatriates. The similarities in operation between both terrorist groups, however, may imply that certain counterterrorism strategies that helped to reduce insurgency in the Niger Delta may also help to reduce insurgency in the north-east if properly executed by morally sound professional handlers concerned with the interests of the nation rather than their selfish motives.

In looking at the national security challenges resulting from insurgency, one can clearly say that all the challenges were caused by those in political offices as well as military commanders who diverted funds for their selfish interests rather that to provide training and ideal equipment to curb terrorism in its infant stages. The security challenges to citizens and foreign nationals have been allowed to spread beyond control and will need strategic planning and implementation going forward.

Some strategies to be applied in combating terrorism in Nigeria include suitable funding and training of the security agencies, strengthening the armed forces with modern and efficient weapons that will effectively outmatch the weapons of the terrorists, and tightening of the Nigerian borders to check the inflow of terrorists into the country. It is important to note at this point, however, that all these recommendations were in place all along. The question here is what exactly is done with the adequate funds pumped in for funding and training of security agents, the sophisticated weapons, and all other tools supposedly supplied for the fortification of security agencies? This funding may only be a continuous cycle of largesse for those in positions of authority, whose turns may have emerged to enrich themselves corruptly. As such, the solution may not be to release more funds into corrupt hands but to first purge the entire system of corruption before other strategies are applied and funds injected into the system.

Insecurity and Socioeconomic Development

The lack of socio-economic development in Nigeria is attributed to security challenges. For Nigeria to enjoy the benefits of development as one geographical entity, the country must be safe and free from insurgency. Insurgency, to a large extent, discourages international investments and local development as potential investors are threatened by insecurity and the danger of losing their investments—and lives, in most cases.

A developmental drive in Nigeria in which the economy is transformed by youth empowerment and development of projects will enhance the economy. It is highly required to engage youths positively and provide the social benefits that will discourage them from being lured into terrorist groups. This supports earlier theories that poverty is the main trigger of sustained terrorism in various forms. It also supports the fact that corrupt practices, mismanagement of resources, as well as lack of visionary leaders have hindered the economic and social development of the nation, thereby creating a loophole for vices that led to grievous consequences such as terrorism. Though the government has in the past made efforts to combat the security situation by allocating more resources to the security budget, as well as passing a bill on antiterrorism, the fact remains that bad governance, lack of well-trained counterterrorists, low morale of troops, corrupt government officials, and above all, a country with deteriorating socioeconomic progression will not yield any positive results in fighting terrorism.

Security and development are two different concepts but are closely related, and they cannot do without each other. This means that in any country where there is conflict, it will be difficult or impossible for development to occur. This implies that for development to be established in any nation, steps must be taken to end conflict and put in place various machineries that will ensure the socio-economic growth of the nation simultaneously.

Although the introduction of social security as one of the ways to create socio-economic development in Nigeria may be helpful, it may be a very difficult project to implement or sustain. Nigeria remains far from this sort of project as issues like sustenance of financing, determination of eligibility, corruption, and other challenges will arise and may puncture the project. In essence, Nigeria is still not ripe enough for such a project. It may even worsen the security situation of the country as vulnerable seniors may be preyed on by youths who expect to get some cash off them after their stipends have been spent. Of course, the stipends paid to youths cannot be sufficient to contain their social vices and general needs. As such, crime may increase, though the initiative may cushion the effects of poverty in the country.

Terrorism and Industrial Development

Recent developments indicate that Nigeria requires economic development as a way of combating terrorism. For Nigeria to be free from terrorism, various stakeholders must be involved in the planning and execution of the strategies that will bring about this freedom. Industrial development of the country, in which government, private sector, civil society, faith, and the international community must be involved in this development to lure foreign investors and enable a conducive environment for investment and business development. The nation's social and economic deprivation has been identified as a probable source for terrorism. In a country where there are no industries developed by foreign investors, jobs will be limited to private enterprises and government. At over 200 million, Nigeria's population suffocates the job market, allowing energetic youths to become vulnerable and accessible to crimes.

Indeed, one of the lapses of the Nigerian government in their bid to tackle terrorism is leaving out other important stakeholders from contributing towards peace in the country. The approach towards counterterrorism in Nigeria has been a single dimensional method in which the military is assigned to engage terrorists through combat. A holistic approach, where civilians in communities affected by terrorism have to be engaged in information gathering, must be achieved. The government, in funding various projects such as education, training, community development, rehabilitation, and deradicalization, must be seen to cover all areas of terrorism eradication and peace impartation which must include industrialization.

Industrial development is a modern society's way of progression and is key to determining the classification of a country. Countries that are placed as underdeveloped, developed, or developing are categorized by their stage of industrial development, which results in the provision of jobs at all levels and the improvement of the country's economy. However, there are many factors that deter industrial development. They include dependence on imported goods, dependence on mineral resources, poor management, corruption, and lack of foresight. In recent times, terrorism has been a major cause of lack of industrial development, especially in countries like Nigeria, where the effect of insurgency is high. This adds to the rate of poverty and provides reasons youths become involved in acts of terrorism. If more jobs can be created for youths, they can be engaged positively, reducing the numbers and strength of terrorists. In turn, this will reduce the effects of terrorism on the nation.

Industrial development, therefore, may be a solution to eradication of terrorism in Nigeria in the long run—if the right steps are taken in this direction, and stakeholders focus on positive outcomes rather than their selfish interests, as has always been the case in Nigeria. Nigeria has kept drifting from industrialization because of its dependence on oil as the major income earner. Most industries that thrived in Nigeria lost their focus and shut down during and after the country experienced the oil boom. The government focused on oil and neglected other income generators, leaving corrupt and incompetent managers to run down the facilities. Today, projects like the Ajaokuta steel rolling mill, the cocoa plant, coal mines, and agricultural industries either operate scantily or do not exist. This, of course, has thrown millions of youths to the streets and created unemployment vacuums, leaving a huge number of youths with no choice but to resort to crimes which have eventually led to various levels of terrorism.

Military-Civilian Relationship in Counter-Insurgency

Although the military claims superiority over Boko Haram in terms of tactics and victories in the battles against insurgency, the military's capability of handling the sect, or even holding on to locations from which they managed to clear Boko Haram, cannot be fully relied on. One disturbing fact is that some strategies that originally should have been adopted by counterterrorists are being used successfully by the terrorist group. Rather than incorporating civilians into the fight against terrorism and gaining relevant intelligence details that may assist the military, civilians are treated like suspects and kept at a distance by the military. Most likely, this is a result of experiences that occurred when terrorists who appeared to be innocent civilians infiltrated the ranks of the military, concealing and detonating explosives. This has resulted in devastating effects which, when looked at critically, one cannot fault the military for taking precautions. However, it is important to note that civilians form part of the tools required to win the battle against terrorists.

Boko Haram, on the other hand, frequently apply this tactic which has helped them gain valuable intelligence used to increase their victories in ambushing the military and civilians. They are recorded to have used civilians as agents of intelligence gathering at locations where they plan to attack. They reportedly have agents within the military, from who they get precise information on troop movements and strategies.

Worst of all is the military's involvement in providing information as well as arms and ammunition for the sect. In 2014, fifteen Nigerian military officers were found guilty of this unthinkable crime.[21] Though they were severely punished, it will not deter others from committing the same crime as there must have been some form of benefits derived from this betrayal of their colleagues. With the low morale as well as the likelihood that some military personnel may share the ideologies of the sect, it is not out of place to assume that the military still has such characters within its ranks.

The huge number of casualties resulting from terrorism, especially of civilians in Nigeria, should be credited to insurgents as well as the military. While insurgents attack locations to cause destruction, the military counter-attack to register its presence in the same locations, unmindful of the safety of civilians in the vicinity. This has resulted in numerous deaths of civilians by the military and indicates that some of its strategies against terrorism should be revisited to avoid amplifying the victory of terrorists.

Another problem with the Nigerian military is its involvement in human rights abuse, where communal punishment is meted on an entire community that is suspected to harbour terrorists. The community is razed by flames, and members of the community are physically abused by the military, even when they are victims of terrorism themselves. This

---

[21] Campbell, J. (2014). *Nigeria's Boko Haram and Heavy Weapons.* Council on Foreign Relations. Retrieved from https://www.cfr.org/blog/nigerias-boko-haram-and-heavy-weapons.

leaves civilians with no option but to flee from communities approached by soldiers in other to be saved from the additional wrath of the military.[22]

One sure way forward in eradicating terrorism in Nigeria is to dissuade the military and its militia's antiterrorism groups from being terrorists themselves. This statement is attributed to the actions of the military, taken in extrajudicial killings of citizens suspected to be terrorists. Amnesty International has several times spoken out on the issue of human rights violations by the Nigerian military, claiming that this action, when adopted as one of their strategies in stopping terrorism, would only frighten civilians and keep them far from terrorists as well as the military. This means that the contributions of community members in fighting terrorism is missing and creates a gap in the counterterrorism process in Nigeria. It therefore would be of utmost importance to have a web of ideas that provides the strategies for resolving terrorism when put together, as suggested by the following diagram.

---

[22] Ogundipe, S. (2018). Why Benue community was set on fire—Nigerian Army. *Premium Times*. Available at https://www.premiumtimesng.com/news/headlines/265643-why-benue-community-was-set-on-fire-nigerian-army.html.

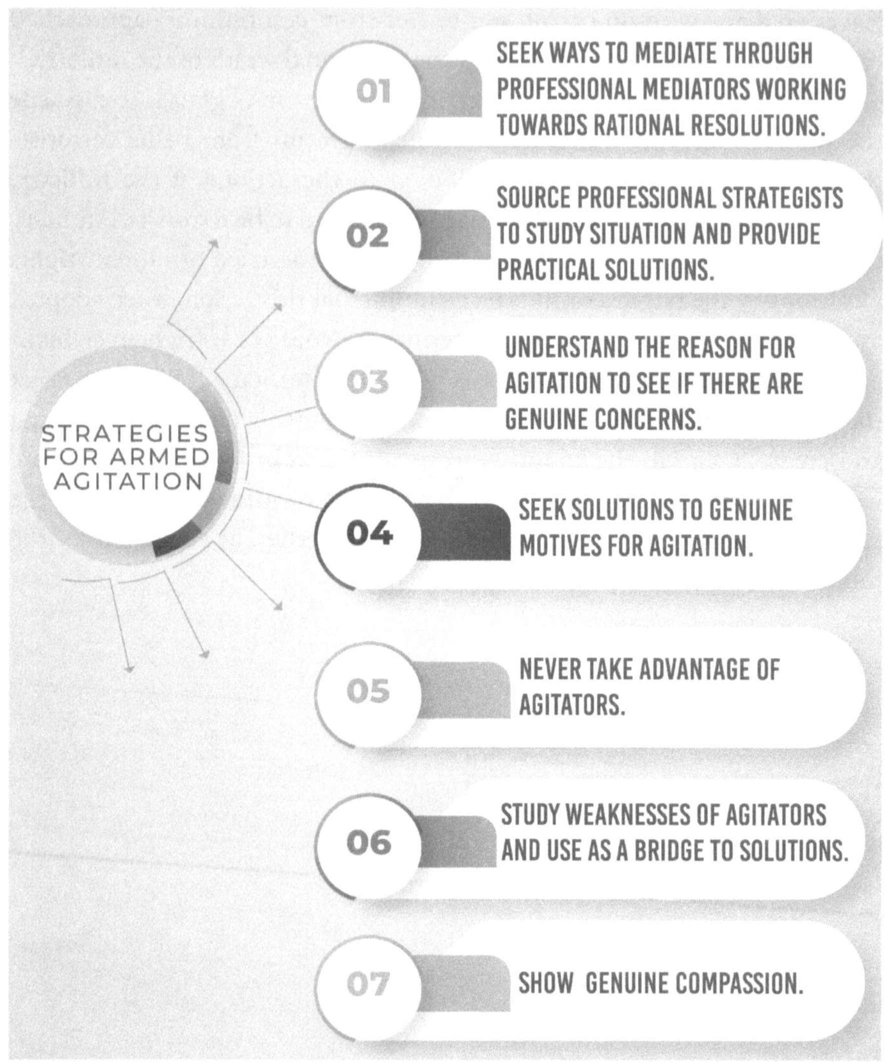

Community Development and Conflict Resolution

One of the major factors fuelling the crisis in the Niger Delta is neglect of the communities by the government as well as foreign industrialists, especially oil companies, who benefit from these communities. The outcry has been that these companies exploit the communities and their people without giving anything in return by technically destroying their means of livelihood. Oil spills have caused destruction of farmlands and rivers in these areas, where farming and fishing remain the only sources of livelihood for the locals. The communities have, therefore, engaged such companies in steady battles for as long as these companies have existed, claiming that little or no consideration and compensation are made or given to them. This has resulted in members of these affected communities picking up weapons. What started as a revolution against the government and the companies degenerated into militancy and full-blown terrorism per the definitions of terrorism by the Nigerian government.[23] The actions of these companies in going to court to fight these communities rather than contributing to the development of the area showed bad faith and resulted in negative actions against them by militant groups.

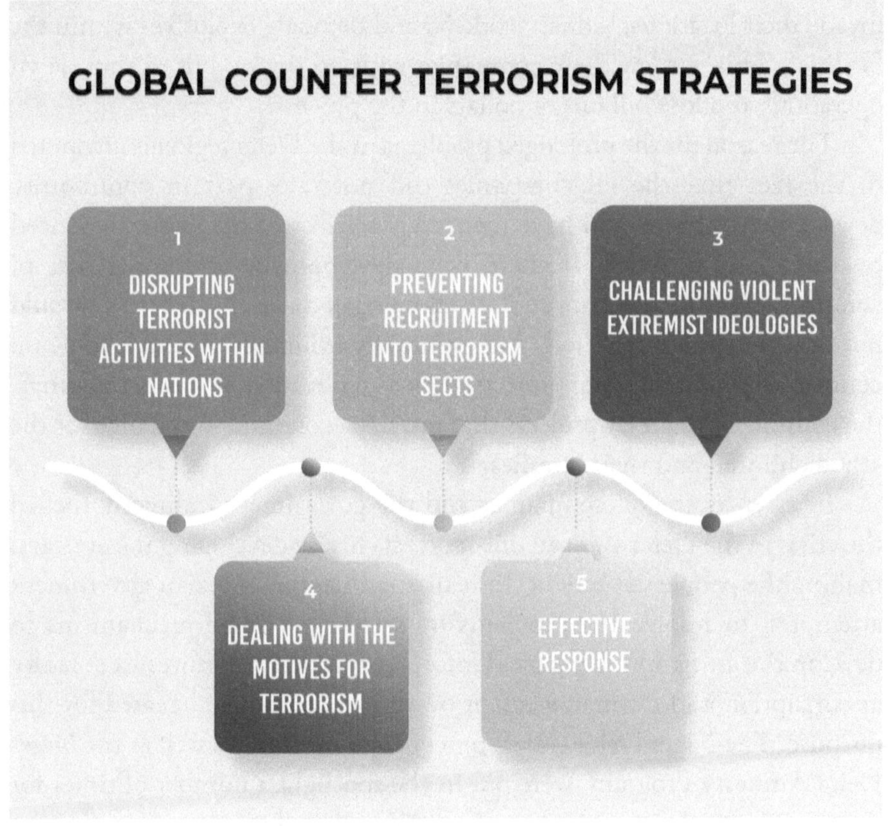

---

[23] Goitom, H. (2011). *Nigeria: Senate, House Approve Anti-Terrorism Bill.* Available at http://www.loc.gov/law/foreign-news/article/nigeria-senate-house-approve-anti-terrorism-bill/.

The Niger Delta militants resorted to kidnapping expatriate oil workers and destruction of oil facilities belonging to these companies and to the Nigerian government. Of course, the government and the companies fought back in the past by using the Nigerian military to show their superiority over the militants. Unfortunately, the military was not trained for battle in the Niger Delta topography and kept falling victim to the militants, who understood their terrain and are experts in manoeuvring in that region. This gave the militants constant victories over the military as well as the government as the nation's economy is always grounded whenever the militants strike. This comes in way of exploding major pipelines that transport petroleum products for export or distribution across the country. The oil companies are not spared in the economic collapse as militants also invade their locations, kidnap workers, and detonate explosives within the facilities. This has left these companies with no option but to shut down operations and lose billions of dollars in the process.

The reason for the prolonged problems in the Delta region is attributed to the fact that the oil companies did not take part in community development, that would have reduced the effect of the loss experienced by these communities. If there were development and some sort of compensation which enhanced the well-being of those affected, there would not be a reason for agitation, and eventually militancy. Though some oil companies execute skeletal projects, such as renovation of school buildings, the communities prefer projects that provide economic sustenance for the schoolchildren and their families.

In essence, the oil companies and the government indirectly fuelled the crisis in the Delta and can only correct this by developing the area and making the people self-reliant. In realizing this, the Nigerian government attempted to resolve the problems by setting up some mechanisms to develop the area and the people. Unfortunately, the structures were faulty as corruption and mismanagement overtook the agencies created for this purpose. The Niger Delta Development Commission, as well as the Niger Delta Amnesty Program, were put in the spotlight a number of times for derailing from their original purposes as well as for corrupt practices by their managements.

The result of this wrong structure has been the training of militants and other indigenous people in vocations that are of little or no use to them. An example is the training of six hundred Niger Delta pilots in South Africa by the Niger Delta Amnesty Program. On return to Nigeria, the pilots had no jobs because they were inexperienced in flying planes available in Nigeria, as well as the limited number of jobs available for pilots in general. Moreover, no Nigerian airline was comfortable with employing ex-militants who were known to have set off bombs across the country and who could hold the airline and passengers at ransom anytime they desired. This indicates that there was no strategic planning involved in carrying out these projects, or the projects' promoters were only after the kickbacks they received from the South African flying schools.

It is important to note that a lot more of these failed educational and vocational projects were carried out in various countries, and billions of dollars were assigned to them with no results. Militants from the Niger Delta region who were trained returned home with no jobs and began another revolution just as it was before embarking on the wasted projects. This failure resulted in the government wasting more resources and reaching an agreement to pay militants monthly stipends for doing nothing and to sustain peace in the region. This financial waste has continued since 2007.

Role of the Military in Combating Terrorism

Strategy development in Nigeria is a task that is assigned to individuals or groups of people who are assumed to be professionals in a particular field. There is no doubt that some of these individuals or groups have come up with strategies that they believe are the best, though these strategies may not be practically applicable to the situations. One of these situations is counterterrorism, and several counterterrorism "experts" have been assigned to provide strategies to combat insurgency in Nigeria.

The general belief about counterterrorism in Nigeria is that the military is well trained and in the best position to advise government on strategies to be taken in that direction. However, the section of the Nigerian military trained as counterterrorists are trained to physically combat insurgents. They do not have the intellectual, strategic knowledge and ability to provide solutions to insurgency based on their training. The best strategy the military can develop in this regard are military tactics and options to further engage insurgents by increasing their strength through the acquisition of more sophisticated weapons, as well as manpower support from within and from foreign military pools.

Some military strategists identify the reasons for insurgency in Nigeria as religious, geopolitical and socio-economical proclivity. They recommend that regarding strategy development, the government should refocus its efforts on counterterrorism by improving border security, enhancing cooperation between all security agencies, improving the physical capability of counterterrorist units, and modifying the criminal justice system in Nigeria. From this, it is obvious that the mindset of the military in Nigeria is focused on engaging insurgents in combat and killing, arresting, prosecuting, and jailing them. These have been the strategies used in Nigeria and have been modified in that same direction over the years.[24]

The actions of the Nigerian military, however, do not conform to modern counterterrorism practices. They have been condemned as non-productive tactics and human rights violations by governments and

---

[24] Udounwa, S. E. (2013). *Boko Haram: Developing New Strategies to Combat Terrorism in Nigeria.* United States Army War College. Available at https://apps.dtic.mil/dtic/tr/fulltext/u2/a590264.pdf.

several organizations, including Amnesty International.[25] These military strategies clearly support the fact that the Nigerian military is trained for combat. While these military strategies are merely a part of the entire process, it is important that other strategies that will ensure the prevention, management, and termination of insurgency must be put in place. There is no doubt that these strategies are useful, but they are clearly for the use by the military in ensuring that they become more formidable in carrying out their combat operations, engaging armed and battle-ready insurgents, while other intellectual and result-oriented strategies should be applied to prevent insurgency and sustain peace and stability.

As part of the strategies being developed to strengthen the military in its role in combating violent extremism, the rank and file of the military require purging. Understandably, troops have complained about poor logistical support. This includes poor feeding, no drinking water, and firepower inferior to that of Boko Haram. This has caused several episodes of mutiny amongst soldiers and must be given urgent attention in the revamping their strategies towards defeating terrorists.

---

[25] Amnesty International (2015). *Nigeria: Senior Members of Military Must Be Investigated for War Crimes.* Retrieved from https://www.amnesty.org/en/latest/news/2015/06/nigeria-senior-members-of-military-must-be-investigated-for-war-crimes/.

Politics and Insurgency

The attitude of policymakers and administrators and the way operations are carried out regarding applied counterterrorism strategies in Nigeria must be redefined if success against terrorists is desirable. It is important to determine if there are internal or external forces—such as the government, policymakers, or administrators—within counterterrorist agencies responsible for the failure of the operations. It must also be determined if a lack of professionalism or the presence of depravities, including corruption, sabotage, and mismanagement of funds, could be attributed to the failure of counterterrorism operatives.

Modern-day counterterrorism involves the use of technology, social development, and combat strategies applied collectively in order to capture every area of attention. It is therefore essential to focus on the examination of strategies, formations, and implementations of workable outcomes to combat terrorism, and the social premises surrounding the avoidance of terrorism and sustenance of peace in Nigeria. It is important that the issue of insecurity is not politicized and for all arms of government to work in unison to achieve the desired goal of providing a safe nation for its citizens.

Recent Research

The deficiency in applied strategies for counterterrorism in Nigeria motivated a research study involving stakeholders engaged in counterterrorist strategies at various levels. Research works that have explored the lived experiences of counterterrorist agents, former terrorists, and victims of terrorism with a view to understanding the strategies being applied in the fight against terrorism in Nigeria reveal the reasons the problem persists after years of terrorist engagement. As a result of the persistent nature of this problem and its global spread, despite several continuous attempts by stakeholders to curb its menace, it was necessary for the author to conduct a study specifically focusing on the strategies applied by counterterrorist agents to neutralize terrorists and eradicate and cushion the effects of terrorism. This groundbreaking research effort was designed to explore the effects of counterterrorist strategies on insurgency in Nigeria. Theoretical frameworks that draw from critical and resource dependence theories were used to aid in recognizing stakeholders' perspectives in relation to social and tactical premises surrounding the application of effective counterterrorism strategies against terrorists operating in Nigeria.

Existing research on counterterrorism continues to hover around the effects of terrorism on society and the development of military or combat strategies against terrorists. The author's study, however, stretched the knowledge on counterterrorism engagement by providing insights on the applied strategies used in combating terrorists and the effects they have on insurgency, with a view to developing workable and more effective approaches.

Participants for the research described their experiences as dumbfounding, disappointing, or a nightmare. The essence of their experiences is to depict the meanings they attributed based on actual accounts of their roles with counterterrorist strategies. This description provides a combination of the textural and structural participant descriptions regarding their experiences. Participants were counterterrorist operatives, victims of terrorism, policymakers, and former terrorists. They shared stories related to their role perceptions, role behaviours, and role performances within the perspective of evaluating counterterrorism strategies. They shared their beliefs, feelings, and thoughts about their roles in or with counterterrorism strategies and suggested that the most important control activity required the development of counterterrorism strategies through training.

Counterterrorist operatives require good knowledge and understanding of their roles in counterterrorist operations to help set clear expectations, recognize unproductive and jeopardizing activities, and ensure intervention is achieved with necessary support. Most participants exhibited a low level of confidence with their organizations and the government. Sharing their experiences, therefore, highlights most of the flaws that may have been concealed from authorities for fear of being reprimanded by higher authorities. If this is addressed, it will result in positive impacts that will be significantly enhanced by increased levels of operative performances.

Each participant understood that counterterrorism operations require supervision and leadership by professionals trained in the act of modern terrorism and counterterrorism studies. Additionally, participants viewed the mitigation of terrorism issues from a performance perspective, combining observation with verbal persuasion. Having a personal commitment to driving performance and an understanding of the responsibility for controlling the act of terrorism are essential for all operatives assigned to such an important task. Participants also considered an understanding of developing effective counterterrorism strategies, along with manpower development and the provision of adequate and necessary supplies, as useful enhancers for performance and effectiveness.

Findings from Recent Research

Current research studies have focused largely on the socioeconomic effects of terrorism in Nigeria, emphasizing its effect on education, culture, economy, and the social well-being of citizens. In terms of counterterrorism strategies applied in curbing terrorism in Nigeria and their effects on insurgency, the findings from the author's recent studies helped spread knowledge on the roles of all stakeholders involved in the fight against terrorism and the development of effective strategies to be used in this process. The symbolic interactionist worldview helped prompt the multiple realisms of participants through interaction and lived experiences, while the symbolic interactionist lens provided the discovery of influences that shaped participants' perceptions about their roles in counterterrorism.

Reviewing the effects of counterterrorism strategies involves a continuous periodic monitoring of operative performance, the use of functional interventions to support and strengthen the goals of operatives, and various blends of ideas developed periodically. The routine of counterterrorist operatives entails daily activities that aid the advancement of a working knowledge of a terrorism framework, as well as knowledge and experience in counterterrorism activities that, in turn, foster the development of effective measures against insurgents.

The results from the author's research provide a window through which other researchers might understand the reasons behind the poor performances of counterterrorist agents and their inability to end terrorism in Nigeria based on their first-hand experiences with the application of the strategies being used. Traditional understanding of counterterrorism in

Nigeria involves the use of military force to engage terrorists in combat. However, findings from recent research prove that engaging terrorists without applying other dynamic tactics is weighty with flaws. There are weak strategies in place complementing combat engagement. Research participants have shared their perceptions on their roles, experiences, and performances within the context of alleviating terrorism in Nigeria.

Major findings have helped to identify and highlight the significance of the roles of all stakeholders involved in the war against terrorism and the recognition of necessities required to equip the actors in counterterrorism to aid efforts aimed at ending the menace. Four key components were identified, resulting in the failure of the existing strategies being applied by counterterrorist operatives and summarized the flaws related to the war against terrorism in Nigeria. They include:

(a) Measuring the performance of counter terrorism agents:

This was the most important component because of the need to assess the performance of operatives and create an understanding that their failure is attributed to a reason. The research results highlighted operatives' experiences and thoughts about their roles in the efforts aimed at curbing terrorism. Counterterrorists' roles involve a stream of detailed and well-structured responsibilities that require urgent intervention from all arms of government, with an aim at reviewing the conditions of operatives which have resulted in them losing the zeal to engage terrorists, as well as the resulting failure in a greater percentage of operations with the same goal. The results revealed that operatives had a low level of morale due to neglect, shortage, or lack of basic and necessary logistic support. This in addition to the poor equipping of combat operatives with tools, machinery, and other equipment required for effective engagement.

(b) Government interventions:

This proved to be an important recipe for success in the fight against terrorism as the government is required to use its human and material resources to intervene in Nigeria's terrorism situation. Operatives complained of neglect and a carefree attitude towards their needs to ensure the effective engagement of terrorists. The various arms of government have their roles to play in the intervention process. Laws must be passed to ensure that strict measures are taken to provide essential tools for operatives. Additionally, laws must be passed to provide strict punitive measures for public officers and those in authority who expose operatives to the imminent dangers of engaging a better equipped terrorist force. The executive arm of government also must ensure it meets all obligations to prepare operatives for engagement with terrorists and to enhance their role performance.

(c) Corruption:

Corruption proved to be an important element negatively impacting the operatives. Findings confirmed that corruption hinders the development of a nation and destroys its citizens even in the midst of wealth. The study revealed that a large chunk of the blame for poor logistic support and lack of proper equipping of operatives is due to perceived corruption among government officials, where hundreds of millions of dollars allocated for weapons and other support materials are diverted to private bank accounts.

Stringent measures must be taken to provide adequately for operatives while safeguarding the nation's financial resources. The government must take advantage of its control of the nation's economy and to be more effective in their obligated role in ending corruption, especially regarding the dangers involved in syphoning funds meant for the fight against terrorism.

(d) Understanding the terrorism framework:

This confirmed the findings suggesting that senior operatives' responsibilities for controlling team members necessitate a clear understanding of terrorism and the counterterrorism framework. The study also proved that operatives have little or no clue about terrorism and the counterterrorism framework and strategic thinking and development of modern tactics that can equate with the knowledge of the terrorists. This knowledge and experience can be obtained through professional training to upgrade the status of operatives to exceed that of terrorists, who continuously update their training. The first step in defeating terrorists is understanding the mind of the terrorist and staying a step ahead. Based on research, it is clear that terrorists change their strategies to throw the military off balance, while the military use the same obsolete strategy of combat engagement as its only means of combating terrorism.

Seven other components were identified when measuring the performance of counterterrorism agents and understanding the terrorism framework. They represented the different elements of experiences embraced by participants during their encounters with the application of counterterrorism strategies by operatives. They are:

(a) Counterterrorism mitigation barriers:

This element revealed that terrorism mitigation barriers adversely impact the role of operatives in curbing terrorism, and that barriers to the mitigation process must be removed. The refusal to remove these barriers implies that the state of security in Nigeria may worsen. Some actors benefit from crisis periods all over the world. In Nigeria, crises are generated or fuelled to sustain an illegal means of financial benefits.

(b) Stakeholder cooperation:

This element depicts participants' beliefs in the need for all stakeholders to work together towards defeating terrorists. As it stands, various organizations are assigned to fight terrorism from different viewpoints. Some vital stakeholders (the community) are not involved in the strategic planning and execution of counterterrorism projects. A challenge is created when there is disunity in a camp or when a team is incomplete. Everyone has a role to play and a strategy that may be effective if it is jointly assessed, refined, and properly executed.

(c) Setting clear expectations:

Observation and verbal persuasion are important mechanisms which positively impact the effectiveness of the role of performance driving acceptable terms to work as a team towards achieving the same goal. This hint indicates that distinct expectations are required to meet specified goals. Through data collection during the author's study, it was clear that some of the commanders are uncertain about what instructions to give troops regarding what they expect. Without proper tools and a high level of morale, it is difficult to set goals. This therefore suggests the need for a multifaceted approach in which troop dynamics are overhauled, and troops are empowered, equipped with strategic goals, and briefed with specific tasks aimed at bringing results.

(d) Understanding roles and obligations:

This emerged as a result of suggestive military authority's disregard by the government. Operatives are of the opinion that the government did not play its role in ensuring that everything needed to end terrorism in Nigeria was provided. The study suggests that the government does not see it as an obligation to end terrorism, and the issue is being handled without serious commitments. As such, government, its officials, and agents are responsible for the peace of citizens and must address their responsibilities and be held accountable.

(e) Using available resources:

This is an important part of equipping operatives with essential tools. A nation's wealth is meant to provide the backing and support it requires for peace and development. Nigeria has natural resources expected to be used as a means of exchange for all the weapons required in fighting terrorism. The government must drive productivity in this area through strategic business deals which will ensure the nation acquires all it needs to maintain peace.

(f) Working with unclear mitigation policies:

Operatives must have a good grasp of their roles in the mitigation of terrorism. Policymakers must come up with clear and useful mitigation policies, void of any political interference. Working with unclear terrorism mitigation policies adversely impacts the operative performances.

(g) Staying current with counterterrorism advancements:

This element impacts the operatives' abilities to mitigate terrorism in Nigeria. Professional advancements continue to transform the lives of humans with increasing levels of integration into day-to-day functioning. An understanding of new professional developments enables practical advancement of new strategies aimed at curbing terrorism. In general, staying current with professional advancements in counterterrorism presents opportunities for a blend of proactive and reactive approaches to mitigation. Professional development in the form of training and capacity building is a necessity for upgrading operatives.

The findings support the view that although the combat personnel trained to engage terrorists play a key role in the drive to eliminate terrorism, other vital roles must be added to their efforts by developing effective strategies, ensuring stakeholders' intervention, and genuine commitment to the fight against insurgency. The key players in the fight against terrorism require a sense of obligation and an understanding of their specific roles and the impact these will cause the nation.

Suggestions for Implementation

This book focuses on gaining an understanding of the strategies used in counterterrorism operations in Nigeria and the reasons they failed to yield positive results many years after the engagement of terrorists by counterterrorist operatives in Nigeria, as well as other supporting West African countries. The interest in exploring the strategies used emanated from the failure of counterterrorism operatives to provide effective solutions for terrorism mitigation. The author's research provided a number of viable and realistic recommendations which can be used in Nigeria and as a template for combating violent extremism and counterterrorism strategies in other countries experiencing terrorism. It is of essence to note that all the stakeholders involved in planning, formulating, and implementing counterterrorism strategies play a significant role in the mitigation of the effects of terrorism on any society. Effective counterterrorism models, such as that which is described in the following table, should be adapted.

In proffering recommendations on this issue, it is important that the welfare of operatives becomes a priority in the fight against terrorism.

MODEL	DEFENSIVE	RECONCILIATORY	CRIMINAL-JUSTICE	WAR
GENERAL FEATURES	Terrorism is regarded as a physical and psychological threat	Terrorism is regarded as a political problem	Terrorism is regarded as a crime	Terrorism is regarded as an act of war
STATE AIMS AND MEANS	Protecting potential targets and victims of terrorist attacks	Addressing the root causes of terrorism	Arrest and punishment of terrorists while adhering to the the rule of law	Elimination of terrorism
CONSTITUTIONAL & LEGAL ASPECTS	In most cases, corresponds with elements of liberal democracy, exceptions can be found when practise undermine civil liberties	Corresponds with the law	The state responds to terrorist incidents in compliance with state criminal law and is subject to constant judicial regulation	Laws of War dictate counterterrorist measures, and constitutional or legal consideration are secondary
AGENTS	Police, private security companies, fire fighters and medical first responders as well as other state and municipal agencies	Policymakers, brokers, diplomats	Police and the criminal justice system	Intelligience and military units

A proper welfare package should be worked out for operatives to ensure that their morale levels are always high. To keep them active should involve a rotational plan be put in place in which operatives are left on the battlefield for eighteen months. This will keep them agile and renew the momentum of attacks every time a new set of operatives is replaced. The welfare package should also include effective fighting tools, vehicles, and combat kitting to ensure that casualty levels are reduced by a considerable percentage, and that the operatives' firepower far exceeds that of the terrorists.

It is also required that operatives are brought up to speed with the knowledge of terrorism and counterterrorism. This provides them with the understanding that other strategies may work better than combat, though physical combat is necessary to protect lives and property of citizens, and to neutralize the terrorist attacks. Through training, knowledge of modern counterterrorism strategies can be acquired so that operatives in situations where they can prevent or de-radicalize terrorists without deadly force, can equally apply them. Terrorists may then reduce their attacks when they realize a refined approach in counterterrorism is being applied.

Counterterrorism communities should also be created across the nation with teams of the military, law enforcement, and the community. This way, vital and fast information will be received, and the best local approach will be used in dealing with the situation. For these communities, periodic training programs should be conducted for upgrade. And in turn, terrorism periodic awareness training programs should also be conducted for other members of the community. These have dual purposes of educating members of the community on how to detect signs of likely terrorist attacks and the steps to take to report to authorities immediately. It will also help in educating the youths to give them enough understanding to have reasons to reject manipulation and attempts at recruiting them into terrorist sects.

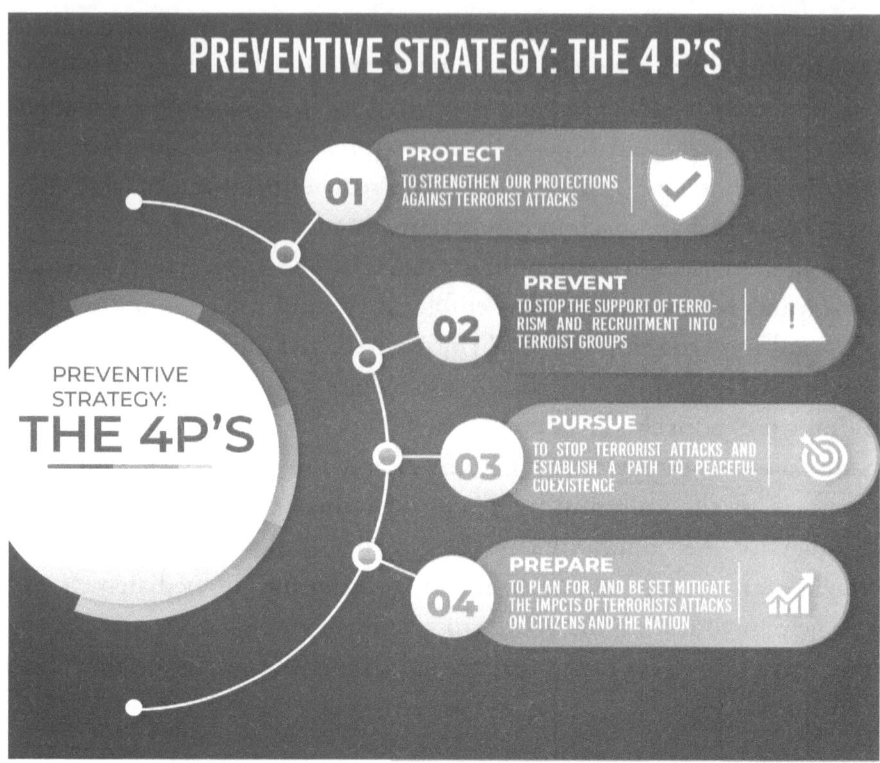

Because poverty and lack of knowledge seem to play a major role in terrorism development, education for children and youths must be provided by the government. Vocational training to empower youths should also be introduced into schools. Islamic schools should have vocational training programs and a monitoring system with government involvement. Because over 53 per cent of children in rural areas only attain a level of education before dropping out to look for trades to learn, this will be a way of providing trades for them early enough for them to become self-reliant.[26] From past experience with the Niger Delta Amnesty Program, careful selection of vocations that will be meaningful to these youths and provide the expected results must be selected.

As a result of the rivalry between the military and other security agencies, a neutral counterterrorist force should be set up with its own

---

[26] UNICEF (2013). *The Challenge: One in Every Five of the World's Out-of-School Children is in Nigeria.* United Nations International Children's Education Fund. Available at https://www.unicef.org/nigeria/education.

well-structured administrative system. Operatives from the armed forces, police, all other security and paramilitary organizations, and members of community watch groups should be neutralized from their services and drafted into this independent and strategically created organization. Intense training and education must be given to provide a new orientation to equip them with the complete understanding of terrorism and counterterrorism, as well as modern strategies to prevent, neutralize terrorism, provide adequate preparation for the mitigation of effects of terrorism acts, and sustain peace in Nigeria.

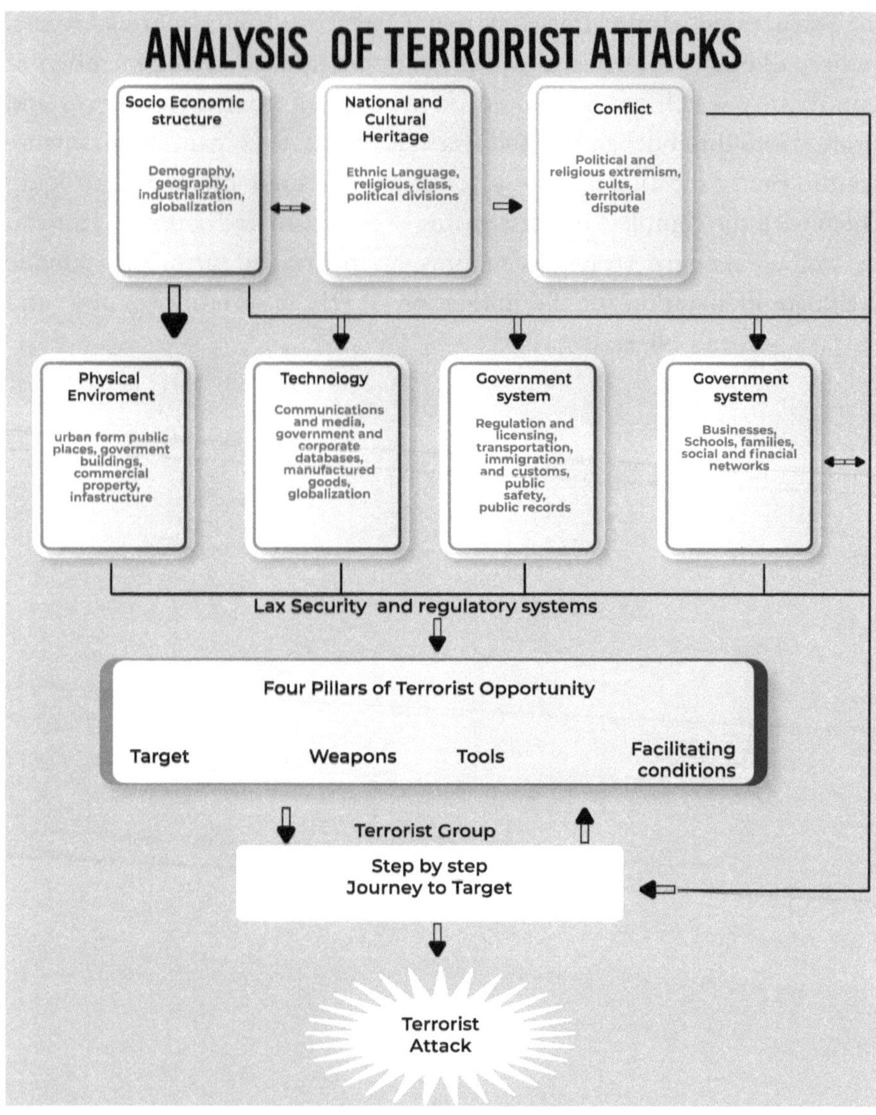

Once all these structures are in place, the government must discontinue negotiations with terrorists that lead to the transfer of wealth to them and their agents. One of the terrorists' strategies when they are low on logistic supplies and cash funding is to kidnap innocent victims for ransom. By providing this cash to terrorists, the government is strengthening their operations, allowing them to survive. A strong stance must therefore be taken by the government to weaken this strategy and make kidnapping less attractive and viable for terrorists.

In strengthening the counterterrorism strategies, the legislature should enact laws that deal decisively with corrupt public officials that divert funds meant for security operations. This will discourage corruption that harms the entire nation. Strict laws, like forfeiture of entire wealth and long prison terms, will serve as deterrents to others. Laws that condemn terrorists should also be enforced to keep them out of the society forever. This will make terrorism less attractive, reduce the population of terrorists, and relegate terrorism to armed banditry, that can be handled by law enforcement.

Due to indications that reasons other than poverty and ideology—such as the effect of climate change, farmers-herdsmen conflicts, boarder disputes, and political rivalry— may be responsible for keeping terrorism ablaze in Nigeria, it would be interesting to research some of the reasons, such as economic factors, where individuals or organizations need to keep the war going in order to sell weapons or other needed war supplies to warring factions. Or in other to gain wealth from resources allocated to security agencies for the restoration of peace. Examining the arms trade and its effects on terrorism will be an interesting subject to research as without armed conflicts globally, manufacturers and traders of weapons will be put out of business.

Impact on Social Change

Professional counterterrorist agents, victims of terrorism, policymakers, and former terrorists have provided opinions and suggestions about how to help in addressing some of the causes of terrorism in Nigeria. Lack of education and intellectual exposure, poverty, and the absence of socioeconomic opportunities for the majority of the youths, especially disadvantaged youths from the north and south of Nigeria, are reasons for the easy recruitment of vulnerable youths and minors into terrorist sects. These suggest that education and empowerment programs should be taken to affected areas to enlighten and educate the youths and help them to understand basic social tenets that will prevent them from being manipulated into terrorism. Empowerment programs (skills acquisition and employment) after education and enlightenment will also be recommended to positively engage the youths and make them self-reliant. This will discourage them from joining terrorist groups as a means of livelihood. With the implementation of these, the society will be safer, and more investments will be established through local and foreign investors, further improving the country's economic situation and providing more jobs. This can be a yardstick or template for other countries in similar situations with gross security challenges. It is hoped that this broadens knowledge on the role each of the stakeholders play either as a barrier or as an effort aimed at mitigating terrorism in Nigeria.

In January 2015, media space was occupied with news of Boko Haram's attack on a military base in northern Nigeria. It was not just an attack but a massive invasion of the military base, that was overrun by the terrorists. In that attack alone, hundreds of victims, including wives and children of soldiers, were either killed or kidnapped by the terrorists.[27] It was an overwhelming blow to the nation and the world at large, especially for those who hid in the comfort of the military strength and perceived ability to control terrorists and their acts.

Today, terrorism has spread beyond the confines of geographical location, religion, and ethnicity. It has almost become a natural phenomenon across Nigeria. Thousands of people are killed and kidnapped for ransom across the country as it appears the nation's counterterrorism forces are not delivering stakeholders' expectations. There is no doubt that the military has numerical and weaponry strength, but in comparison to terrorists who have overtaken Nigeria, they appear to be no match. Reports have it that soldiers flee from the battlefield and disengage from military service for fear of terrorists.[28] This suggests that the terrorists are more advanced in technique, firepower, and numbers.

---

[27] Suleiman, M. L. (2015). Countering Boko Haram. *Counter Terrorist Trends and Analyses* 7(8). Available at https//.jstor.org/stable/26351382?seq=1#metadata_ info_tab.

[28] AlJazeera News (2014). Boko Haram seizes town after soldiers "Flee". *News Africa.* Retrieved from https://www.aljazeera.com/news/africa/2014/08/boko-haram-seizes-town-after-soldiers-flee-2014826181311739107.html.

In analysing the cost of damages and losses to Nigeria's economy, one would say billions of dollars have been lost through the human resources brought down by the terrorists. Also, economic sabotage through the disruption of business activities, monies collected from government as compensation in consideration for discontinuing terrorism or as ransom in exchange for kidnapped victims, and the overall destruction of infrastructure, lives, and properties account for losses. It is in this view that all eyes are focused on counterterrorism agencies assigned to combat terrorism as well as other stakeholders—such as government, policymakers, high authorities of security forces and counterterrorism agencies, and the community—tasked to ensure that the job of effectively fighting terrorism in Nigeria is carried out efficiently.

Despite the adoption and deployment of policies and technical mechanisms against its existence, terrorism continues to persist. The results of the effects of existing strategies on performance by counterterrorism operatives require the augmenting of these strategies with more effective ones to enhance overall performance. It was necessary to look deep into the reasons the existing strategies fail and follow through with the recommendations made to work out ways in which effective ones may be developed to liberate Nigerians from the chains of terrorism. It is permissible to admit that most of the problems related to the impact of terrorism on the nation are consciously generated problems imposed on the nation by those who were elected and appointed to govern and administer policies. Among other issues, it has been unravelled that high-level corruption, lack of developmental training of personnel, lack of knowledge of terrorism and the counterterrorism framework, lack of an upgrade in combat tactics carried out by the military, and poor level of operative morale were reasons for the failure of operations as well as the deterioration of the military might.

The gap between evidence of the effectiveness of counterterrorism strategies and the enforcement of counterterrorism policies may be due to poor supervision of those assigned to check the activities of policymakers and senior executives of the counterterrorism agencies. Though few studies have focused on the adequacy and effectiveness of strategies used by counterterrorism operatives aimed at mitigating the different typologies of terrorism, the author has attempted to explore the effects of counterterrorism strategies on insurgency and the roles as well as the experiences of stakeholders during the engagement of terrorists.

It is necessary to develop counterterrorism strategies that support the need for stakeholders to consider redefining their approaches to the problem in Nigeria. However, to make this come to fruition, the cooperation of all entities involved, as mentioned previously, must be encouraged to come together as one strong team to work out effective strategies and remedies to end terrorism, eliminating self-interest and to put the nation first.

At this point, credit must be given to the Nigerian army for their genuine interest in ensuring peace through the fight against terrorism in Nigeria. Between 2019, when a copy of the author's dissertation was submitted to the leadership of the Nigeria army, and the time of this publication, some of the strategies discussed in the dissertation and in this book have been visited by the military and are being given consideration. The dissertation, titled *Evaluating the Effects of Counterterrorism on Insurgency in Nigeria*, presently sits in the Tukur Buratai Institute for War and Peace library in Biu, Nigeria, and is also published online. However, it is important that these newly introduced strategies, as well as others that have been discussed, are thoroughly studied, understood, developed, and applied to suit the diverse nature of terrorism in various parts of the country. Notable among the strategies visited is the collaboration with community members through the formation and joint operations with civilian vigilante groups and local hunters known as the Civilian Joint Task Force (CJTF).

A new wave of terrorism has begun in Nigeria. Unfortunately, there is only one motive: to gather wealth in any way possible. Various groups have sprung up, terrorizing citizens and the government by kidnapping vulnerable citizens and securing their release with huge ransoms. In some cases, the victims are killed even after these ransoms have been collected. Following the definition of terrorism in Nigeria, it is right to say that the new wave of terrorism is sweeping across the country rapidly.

2 | Incentivized Comfort Terrorism

Whenever terrorism is mentioned, our thoughts go to how terrorists are financed to sustain the existence of the sects and fund their operations. This is a vital part of terrorist operations, and terrorists have devised various methods to generate revenue for their organizations' sustenance. Bearing in mind that terrorism is an enterprise because a lot of intellectual and financial capital are invested in it, income, revenue, and interests are expected to be yielded from this sort of investment. Strategies for generating and sustaining income must also be renewed to meet with the demands of terrorists. While terrorists generate funds through illegal activities such as bunkering, looting, armed robbery, kidnapping, sales of contraband goods, and money laundering, their return on these investments include capital funds in terms of money from ransoms, government compensations, and funding by interested parties, as well as deaths, fame, anguish, destruction, horror, and social retrogression. As weird as these may seem, these are the expectations and the sources of delight of every terrorist.

While we understand that money is required to keep terrorism alive, this topic focuses on how terrorists also switch emphasis of their motives from religious ideology, deprivation, and other reasons to making unmeasurable wealth for themselves and their families. For clear illustration, the spotlight is on the Niger Delta militants and insurgents from northern Nigeria (terrorist groups and bandits, who have recently been listed as terrorists by the government of Nigeria), who have all found wealth and comfort from terrorism and used this as a measure for peace and stability in their various regions.

Common knowledge has it that the motive behind the agitation in the Niger Delta region hinges on concerns connected to deprivation, marginalization, and neglect of a region generating wealth for the nation while its people wallow in abject poverty. This was the general focus when the likes of Isaac Adaka Boro and Ken Saro-Wiwa fought for the emancipation of the people of the Niger Delta. The only compromise at that time was death. It was either they were killed by the government or they fight on till the suffering of their people came to an end. Unfortunately for these two great men, they paid the ultimate price for their struggle since the government was unprepared to change its stand on the position of the people of the Niger Delta. Both men were killed in different circumstances. While Boro was released from prison to fight for the Nigerian troops during the civil war in 1969, where he lost his life in unknown circumstances in 1969, Saro-Wiwa was executed by hanging in 1995 by the Sani Abacha regime in Port Harcourt.

The new-generation "freedom fighters" from the Niger Delta were mostly young men without a direct focus but a sense of entitlement. While riding on the existing motive created by Isaac Boro and Ken Saro-Wiwa, their modes of operation differed from that of their so-called mentors, who used little physical and more intellectual warfare as fighting tools against the Nigerian government. The new breed, however, developed a strategy that hit the government directly below the belt. It is believed that because their motives had a business undertone, strategies to ensure that the Nigerian government go on its knees were developed and applied. Notwithstanding the damages and repercussions to the land and people of the Niger Delta, these militants, as they were known, blew up oil pipelines without consideration of its outcome to the nation's economy.

Expatriates were also targets for kidnapping for ransom, and piracy and robberies were the order of the day. Although their targets for robbery were bullion vans carrying money and banks where monies were insured, the militants claimed these calculated targets had no adverse effect on citizens.

Other than self-exploitation, these militants have applied various other means to enrich themselves.

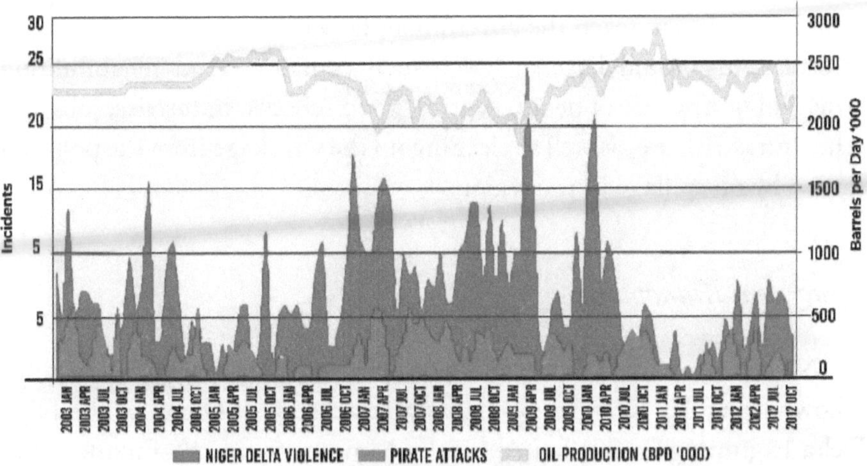

Diagram showing violence in the Niger Delta vs effect on oil production.

Financial Empowerment Structure of the Niger Delta Militants

Self-Exploitation

Some of the major actors in the Niger Delta incentivized comfort terrorism scheme are Mujahid Asari-Dokubo, Government Ekpemupolo (aka Tompolo), Ateke Tom, Henry Okah, and Ebikabowei Victor-Ben (aka Boyloaf). These were the leaders of various factions in the region and should take responsibility for actions taken under their command. At the beginning, there were huge signs of genuine intentions in their actions to emancipate their people from the unjust treatment of the Nigerian government. In 2003, Asari Dokubo, retreated into the bush to form the Niger Delta Peoples Volunteer Force (NDPVF) with the clear motive of gaining control of petroleum resources, the major income earner of the nation. This goal was attempted through oil bunkering, an illegal method through which oil pipelines are tapped, and the products are diverted onto a barge for sale on the black market in Africa and the West. As militants made efforts to justify their actions because the Nigerian government had exploited the region for decades, one would think their genuine intentions of forcefully getting unexploited would be to use the proceeds from bunkering to teach the government how the region should be taken care of. This would have included such things as road rehabilitation, provision or upgrade of health centres, good schools, industries, jobs, and other infrastructure, as well as cleaning up the wreckage from the pollution caused by oil spillage in the region.

Piracy and Kidnappings

Nigeria was named the second-worst nation in Africa involved in piracy following regular activities of high sea attacks by militants of the Niger Delta beginning in 2012. Led by the Movement for the Emancipation of the Niger Delta (MEND), militants hijacked twelve ships, kidnapped thirty-three sailors, and killed four oil workers. Numerous foreign oil company employees have been taken hostage. Over two hundred foreigners have been kidnapped since 2006 and released after huge ransoms were collected. Again, these ransoms were not used to develop the region. Rather than socio-economic development, the region kept experiencing social and environmental degradation caused by continuous oil spills, military counteractions, and lack of government attention. Also, because oil companies were constantly attacked in various ways and extorted, corporate social responsibility by multinational companies within communities in the Delta seized.

INCIDENCE OF TERRORISM ACROSS NIGERIA

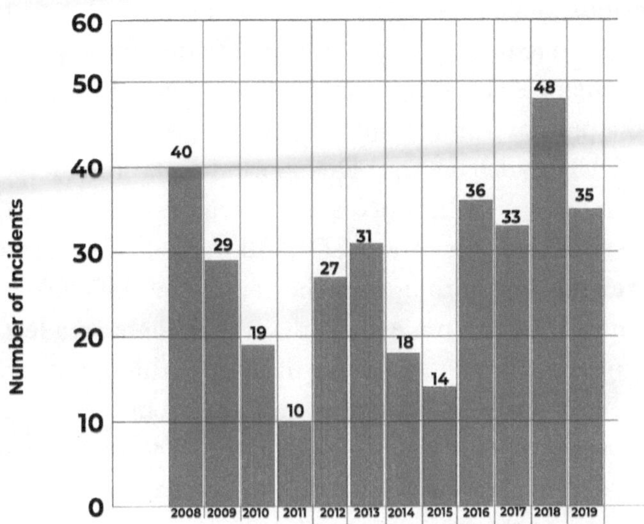

Diagram showing the level of sea piracy in Nigeria.

Other Sources of Wealth

Militants also made revenue off politicians in all states of the Niger Delta in Nigeria. This was in favour of sustenance of peace or for assistance in the manipulation of election processes by politicians. State governors, the federal government, political parties, and individuals were part of those that gifted militants huge sums of money for the above reasons. With so much wealth contributed into the wallets of people who blamed the government of deprivation, it would have been expected that some sort of development in the region would begin. Regrettably, no projects were carried out by these militant groups to prove a point to government and to fix the problem of abandonment of infrastructural development in the Delta region.

The Cash for Arms Deal

In 2004, the Nigerian government agreed to address some of the political demands made by Niger Delta militants. In exchange for this, the militants agreed to hand over their weapons to the federal government. However, the handover of weapons came with another price. Leaders of the NDPVF and a pro-government militia group known as the Niger Delta Vigilantes (NDV), headed by Asari-Dokubo and Ateke Tom, respectively, were the first to enjoy the largesse of this executive deal. Thousands of weapons were exchanged for cash. USD1,800 was paid for each rifle at a time when the same sort of rifles could be bought for USD200.

The real deal with this project was that the militants made a fool of the government and amassed wealth for themselves through this dubious peace accord. Weapons were bought by militants from arms dealers and sold to the government for a USD1,600 profit. The project lasted for many months, giving militants the window to purchase as many weapons as possible for sale to the government while keeping their weapons. The total count at the end of the exercise was not made public, but thousands of weapons were said to have been "collected" from the militants.

The Niger Delta Development Company (NDDC)

Although the Niger Delta Development Commission (NDDC) was established by former president Olusegun Obasanjo with a focus to develop the petroleum-rich Niger Delta region, since its commissioning, the NDDC has attempted to concentrate on the development of social and physical infrastructures, devotion to ecological and environmental rehabilitation, as well as human development. Whereas the NDDC was created primarily to cater to the demands of the people of the Niger Delta, this was and is still a source of wealth for militants. The militants and political authorities within this region have always hijacked the bulk of the juicy contracts from the NDDC. Most of these contracts, running into billions of US dollars, were fully paid for but never executed, leaving observers with no other rational views than the fact that the NDDC has been and is a cash cow for militants and politicians, while the region remains underdeveloped.

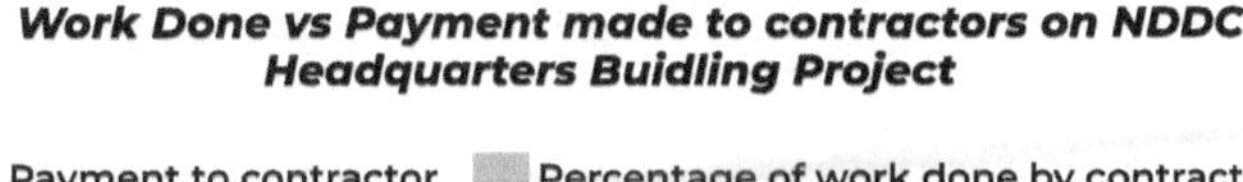

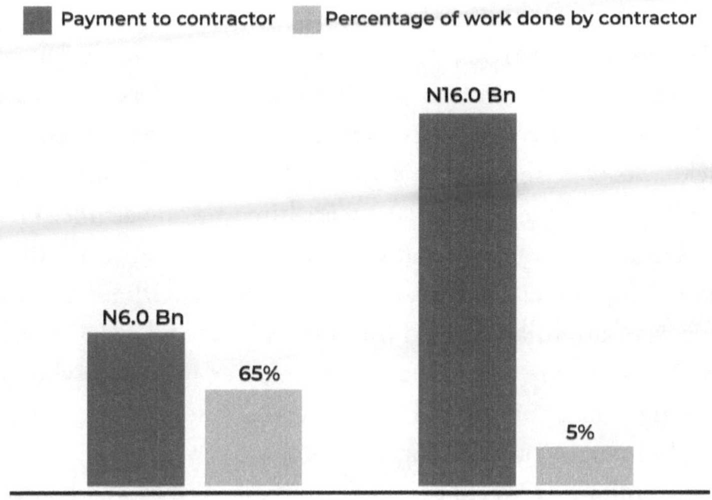

Diagram showing the level of corruption in NDDC.

Presidential Amnesty Program

As a result of the steady pipeline attacks during the insurgency in the Niger Delta, and the huge negative economic impact it had on the nation, the Nigerian government was forced to grant amnesty and unconditional pardon to all militants on June 26, 2009, in exchange for peace in the region. The presidential amnesty program focused on training ex-militants. It also opened more doors for corruption and enrichment of Niger Delta militant leaders. Because of the viability of this so-called business venture, militant leaders who had foresight led their groups to actually surrender weapons such as rocket-propelled grenades, rifles, explosives, ammunitions, and gunboats to the government. The benefits that came from this gesture included huge contracts to secure the waterways for insurgents in a country with a strong navy. Monthly stipends were to be paid to over 30,000 ex-militants through assigned militant leaders, and overseas training of militants at various levels were established. Thousands of militants were sent to universities and vocational training centres, that were established in a hurry, to funnel funds from the amnesty program. They were owned by militant leaders.

The main goal for those whose intentions were to make money from this project was to send as many students as possible to courses that favoured the managers of the projects and militant group leaders. An example of this are the six hundred students trained as pilots in South Africa, while huge kickbacks were received by the handlers through vendors. On their return to Nigeria, none of the pilots were hired by any airline. First, they had only basic pilot training that did not qualify them to fly the sort of planes in the commercial or private pool in Nigeria. Airlines and airplanes in Nigeria were also fully engaged with professional and experienced pilots. And finally, no airline would want to employ ex-militants who, prior to their training as basic pilots, had been involved in several acts of terrorism, including kidnapping and killing.

For the militants who got the opportunity to travel abroad on airplanes for the first time in their lives, this was a major breakthrough. An additional benefit of monthly stipends for doing nothing became the high point of the national largesse at their level, while their leaders went home with millions of dollars at the expense of the development of the Niger Delta and its people.

This is not to say that some indigenes did not benefit from this program. Most of the beneficiaries in the higher education program were not directly militants but relatives, friends, and romantic associates of militant leaders and project handlers. While these categories took the slots of the real militants, the number of untrained militants and their monthly compensations remained static.

S/N	Institutions	Course	No. of Delegates	Location	Status
1	Schlumberger Tehnologies	Drilling Engineering	29	Melon, France	Graduated
2	Lufthansa Aviation Academy	Instrument Rating, Type Rating and Fixed Wings	21	Frankfurt, Germany	In Training
3	CAE Oxford Aviation Academy	Airline Transport Instrument rating, Type Rating	9	Kinglington, UK	In Training
4	Schneider Electric	Power Generation & Management, process and machine management	29	France	Graduated
5	Institute of French Petroleum (IFP)	Geoscience, Reservoir Engineering, Gas Exploration, Production, Refining, Engines & Hydrocarbon Utilizations	40	France	In Training
6	Airstar Flight School	Helicopter	9	Italy	In Training
7	Comair	Type Rating	11	South Africa	In Training
8	Flight Simulation Company	Type Rating	4	Netherlands	In Training
	TOTAL		**152**		

Source: OSAPND in Moshood (2016)

Table showing some programs undertaken by militants.

The Presidency of Goodluck Jonathan

The presidency of Goodluck Jonathan came with a sense of entitlement for militants of the Niger Delta, especially because the president was their kinsman, and they were being pampered at that time. To sustain the existing peace accord inherited by Jonathan, the government under him had to celebrate the militant leaders, sustain their benevolence, and extend a hand of good gestures by appointing their friends, relatives, and allies to juicy government agencies such as the Nigerian Maritime Administration and Safety Agency (NIMASA). Patrick Akpobolokemi, an alleged relative of Government Akpomupolo (Tompolo) was appointed director general of this salacious agency that awarded contracts worth millions of US dollars to Global West Vessel Specialists Nigeria Limited (GWVSNL), a company owned by Tompolo. This contract was to last ten years. GWVSNL was assigned to protect Nigerian waterways and ensure the safety of local and international vessels amongst other responsibilities. Other agencies, as well as federal and state ministries, also awarded sumptuous contracts to militant leaders in the Niger Delta, aiding them in their plots to grab wealth and live in luxury. Most of their investments were sited far from the Niger Delta region, some abroad, some in Abuja (the nation's capital), and others in neighbouring West African countries.

Threats and Pipeline Explosions

To maintain the steady flow of crude oil, the government and oil companies have continually bowed to the threats of militants. In February 2016, an explosion in a pipeline operated by Shell Petroleum Development Corporation's Forcados export terminal ceased production and importation. This explosion occurred for the first time after the peace deal brokered between militants and the Nigerian government, in 2009. This act dropped the production to 300,000 barrels a day as a result. On May 11, 2016, Shell closed its oil facility in Bonny as three soldiers on guard were killed in an attack. A week earlier, a bomb explosion had shut down Chevron's Escravos GTL facility. On May 19, 2016, ExxonMobil's Qua Iboe facility also shut down, and its workers were evacuated as a result of militant threats.

As the Niger Delta Avengers (NDA), a newly formed militant group in the Niger Delta, declared its presence in March 2016, it became obvious that it had orchestrated attacks on oil-producing facilities, causing the oil terminals to shut down and triggering a fall in Nigeria's oil production. For the first time in twenty years, the attacks caused Nigeria to fall behind Angola, which then became Africa's largest oil producer. Since Nigeria depends mainly on the oil industry for the bulk of its government revenue, the reduced oil output hampered the Nigerian economy and destroyed its budget.

The government's constant indulgence has provided militants with the stimulus to threaten and blow up pipelines. Just as terrorists and bandits in the north of Nigeria use kidnapping and trading of schoolchildren (especially girls) as their contrivance for negotiation with the government, the militants have also discovered that threats and pipeline destruction have become their means for financial extortion and negotiation with the Nigerian government.

In August 2016, the NDA declared a ceasefire and agreed to negotiate with the Nigerian government. Of course, some militants were heavily compensated with contracts and monetary gifts to ensure the pipelines remained intact and oil production recommenced. After the NDA declaration of a ceasefire, other militant groups—such as Reformed Egbesu Fraternities (comprising the Egbesu Boys of the Niger Delta, Egbesu Red Water Lions, and Egbesu Mightier Fraternity)—were carried along and benefitted from the negotiations, announced a ceasefire.

Because of the romance with the government, it is easy for any individual or group of persons in the Niger Delta to form a militant group and engage the government with threats. Since it has always worked for them and brought wealth to their doorsteps, it should be expected that when leaders of the known militant groups get broke, there will be new threats on the oil pipelines in the Niger Delta.

When youths get hungry, there will also be threats or actions against Niger Delta oil facilities with the hope that negotiations with the government will bring them the much-desired wealth. This is evident by the August 9, 2016, declaration of the existence of Justice Mandate, another new group that threatened to destroy refineries in Port Harcourt and Warri, as well as a gas plant in Otu Jeremi. The next day, the group reportedly blew up a major oil pipeline operated by the Nigerian National Petroleum Company (NNPC) in Isoko. On August 12, 2016, the group warned that it would blow up additional oil installations, and on August 19, 2016, they purportedly detonated two pipelines belonging to Nigerian Petroleum Development Company (NPDC) in the Delta state. On August 30, 2016, the Ogor-Oteri oil pipeline was exploded by the same group. On 4 September, the group claimed that all marked oil and gas facilities had been rigged with explosives and warned residents living near them to evacuate.

The question now is why didn't they carry out their threats, and why are they no longer threatening the government? The answer isn't far-fetched as the tradition of gifting militant leaders with fat contracts and money must have taken place. This circle of events will continue as long as the government keeps giving in to the demands of militants in the Niger Delta. Strategies must be developed to prevent militants from sabotaging the nation's economy. This strategy must involve education and training on the importance of preserving national investments, the need for social and economic development across the country, and the actual empowerment of the youths of the region to ensure that they have no need to vandalize pipelines.

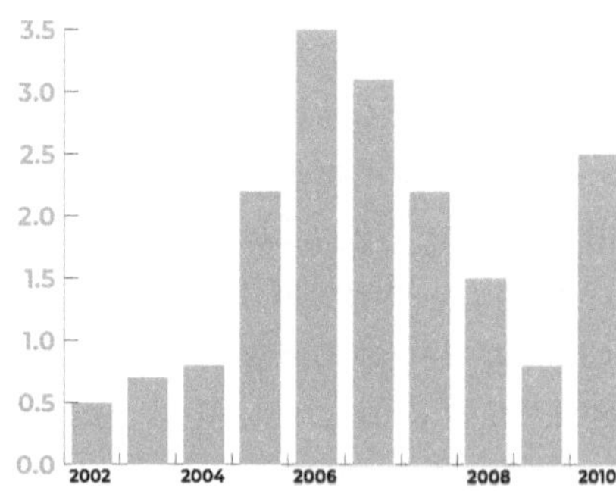

Diagram of pipeline attacks in the Niger Delta.

Community Counterterrorism Initiative

Dislodgement and Migration of Terrorists: The Threat

For decades, the Boko Haram terrorist group has held Nigeria sway with their frequent attacks on the civilian population and military formations. The war against terrorism in Nigeria takes different dimensions with either side oppressing the other. At times, terrorists are being defeated and forced deeper into their fortress in Sambisa Forest. The forest's thick vegetation is large enough to accommodate the huge number of insurgents as well as their abductees. It also provides ideal camouflage for their well-equipped armoury and logistics storage.

As promising as it seems that the threats of Boko Haram are fast ending whenever the military appears to be winning the battle, the defeat of these insurgents always generates another phase of terrorism even closer to the communities. As the government of Nigeria focuses on its ultimate plan to dislodge the insurgents from the forest, a vital concern for the government should be the fact that if the insurgents are dislodged from their fortress, they will be inevitably spilled into various communities around the country, thereby producing multiple cells of terrorist groups in cities across Nigeria and West Africa. The implications of this are widespread terrorism and more frequent attacks on communities. This will amplify terrorism, put more lives in danger, cause a downward slope in development, and generously spread the impact of terrorism on more people and communities.

Potential Impact

The impact of this potential problem cuts across all ages and genders, as well as all classes of people living within these areas of terrorist migration. The communities where they are likely to resettle are of all sorts and ranges. For them not to be easily noticed, however, their choices will be more in low- and average-income earning communities. They will nevertheless infiltrate the high-income earning communities as night watchmen, drivers, and other kinds of domestic employees. This means that all kinds of communities are vulnerable to attacks due to the presence of insurgents who can be used at any time to commit a terrorist act that will affect individuals, families, and communities at large in the following ways:

(a) Short Term Psychological Impact

The immediate problems and psychological challenges that will be faced are the thoughts of insecurity within the communities. Even as parents fear for their own safety, the safety of their children will also be a great concern as they will have to be separated while at work or at school. Their fears do not only edge around the fact that physical terrorist attacks can occur in their communities but also for the fear of the agony they may face if their children or females are kidnapped and used as domestic and sex slaves for the insurgents. The ease with which this can occur is being created by the envisaged problem.

(b) Long-Term Psychological Impact

The long-term psychological impact of this problem would be various levels of mental disorder, such as acute stress disorder (ASD) and post-traumatic stress disorder (PTSD) caused by trauma from various bitter experiences that may occur during potential acts by these terrorists. One example is the effect of students not being able to meet up with peers who continued school while they are abducted and in captivity. The case of 276 female students abducted from their secondary-school dormitory while preparing for their final exams in the Chibok local government area of Borno state in Nigeria by Boko Haram on April 14, 2014, remains an example. Two escaped from captivity the day of the attack and were sent to the United States for rehabilitation and further studies by the Nigerian government. These two lucky survivors have had the opportunity to start new lives in America and earned graduate degrees. Their colleagues, who had been in captivity for close to three years, were eventually released and returned to their parents. They did not, however, have the same measure of rehabilitation given to the ones in America. It is obvious that they will not be able to match up with their friends who are getting close to being professionals in various fields with totally different social statuses and global exposure.

The feeling of being a victim, carrying a child for one of the insurgents is another concern as victims will have to deal with some form of stigmatization within the community. This may lead to relocation from the community, away from loved ones who are meant to help in the recovery process, resulting in further psychological damage. The fear of degenerating psychological problems leading to full mental conditions exists because of the poor state of medical facilities in Nigeria. Again, dealing with patients with mental conditions in Nigeria is different than in much of the West. Patients are chained and given inhumane treatment in some communities which, of course, gives great concern to people of the communities at risk as they consider what may lie ahead for them in terms of the victims turning against their own communities.

(c) Neurobiological Impact

The neurobiological impact of the potential problem will be a nervous breakdown due to the stress disorders that may arise from the attacks and the effects of the attack on communities. Once one attack occurs, there will be fear of multiple attacks around other communities infiltrated by terrorists. The results will be hallucinations in anticipation of the next act, high risk of contracting ASD and PTSD, and the effects of degenerating neurological conditions as a result of incapable medical crisis workers.

(d) Behavioural Impact

Individuals and families will become very apprehensive of strangers and their environment as everyone and everything may seem suspicious. Generally, the community will develop an unfriendly atmosphere, and law enforcement may become strict in their fight against domestic terrorism. Owing to the history of law enforcement brutality of innocent citizens suspected to be terrorists, there will be fear amongst people, leading to a restriction of their movements and social activities, or even sporadic attacks by citizens on law enforcement.

(e) Cognitive Impact

The Boko Haram sect has the ideology that Western education is bad. It therefore means that if insurgents from this group live amongst communities, students of Western education will continue to be prime targets as witnessed today. Of course, the effect of this is that a lot of schools will close, and students will withdraw from school, causing a fracture in the educational system as well as the overall quality of the youths based on their poor educational status. It will also be easier for them to achieve their goal of turning West African countries into caliphates, first by putting fear into citizens, then forcing them to accept their faith, and finally, take part in acts of terrorism. These terrorists are unlikely to face any meaningful opposition since Nigeria has strict weapon laws, and weapons for citizens to fight against these sects are not readily accessible, even when the military may not be available to cover certain areas. When the weapons are available, citizens may not have the basic training to combat insurgency.

(f) Impact on Special Populations

The special population is the most vulnerable in this situation. They include first responders, children, the disabled, and the elderly. As a result of their unique situations that require some form of physical assistance, the actual impact of terrorist acts may affect them more.

First responders are usually the people or organizations that are first to arrive at crisis locations. In the case of Nigeria and the communities within, the major impact on this group will be the fear of coming in contact with remnant terrorists or undetonated explosives. Cases have occurred in which first responders were hit by explosives. Another problem is the risk of contracting certain viruses—like HIV, hepatitis, and Ebola—as a result of being under-equipped to carry out delicate crisis management jobs in which body parts and fluids are littered around.

Children are at risk of being hit by explosives when they are away from their parents' care. They also are at risk of being kidnapped by terrorists in exchange for ransom or to be forcefully recruited into terrorism sects. They risk starting lives as terrorists, thereby endangering themselves as they automatically become enemies of the state and, therefore, be exposed to military counteractions. It has become common to see children used as suicide bombers for terrorist groups in Nigeria. Most of them were kidnapped from rural areas close to the forests. This process of kidnapping and radicalizing children will be repeated constantly to continue their style of attack.

The disabled are another group that require human support for mobilization and welfare. In normal circumstances, many can hardly fend for themselves. The well-to-do disabled population may not be in this category as they can afford different means of escaping physical harm. Those who will be affected mostly are disabled street beggars and those from very humble homes. Apart from physical attacks on them, there will face psychological issues, such as the fear of being left at the mercy of terrorists when the potential attack eventually comes. Those who survive will also have a problem being attended to as they are seen as second-class citizens in Nigeria, and crisis workers will not attended to them when there are able-bodied victims in need of their attention.

The elderly, in a crisis situation, may hinder smooth movement of others and reduce chances of survival for their caregivers. Their caregivers need to decide whether to remain with the elderly they care for and face the risk or seek protection for themselves. Meanwhile, the elderly are gripped with fear of the unknown and the result of the impending attack on their communities. Some of them already have medical conditions such as PTSD from previous stressors. This new fear may either cause a relapse in their already fragile condition or lead to fatal conditions.

The Media and Terrorism

Media coverage of any activity has its importance. It also has negative and positive impacts on viewers as well as on those directly concerned with the story. The negative impact of media coverage on terrorism, however, outweighs the positive impact as it tends to favour the terrorists. In most cases, the media tend to overhype stories in order to market their news articles. By doing this, there is the tendency to give terrorists an undeserved advantage over governments and citizens, bearing in mind that the more people their messages or threats reach, the more successful the terrorists.

Terrorists aim at intimidating their targets through threats to create fear and recruit members. The easiest way to achieve this is through the media as all television and radio stations, as well as online and print media houses, rush to spread stories on acts of terrorism or threats by terrorists. Unfortunately, these stories are repeated for weeks, giving the terrorists the free publicity they desire. Though reporting these stories may alert authorities and provide measures for preventing terrorist attacks or for proper intervention and post-attack plans, the damage it causes to the psychological well-being of the populace ends up working in favour of terrorists, who may apply the weakness of the media as one of its strategies for committing psychological warfare.

Of course, it is important that media cover and report terrorist activities to either warn citizens of the dangers that exist in particular locations or the progress made by law enforcement in tackling them. However, media reports must be limited to basic information, such as the location where an act of terrorism was carried out, and the fact that emergency personnel have been dispatched to contain the situation. Further reports should include areas of presumed danger and feedback on investigations and the outcomes of law enforcement actions against terrorists. Research shows that different types of terrorist actions have different media impacts. It was found that suicide missions get considerably more media coverage than any other form of terrorist attack, which explains the increasing popularity of this sort of attack among terrorist groups. There is, therefore, a need to readdress the startling coverage of terrorism and to stop providing terrorists a free media platform to showcase their cruelty, thereby creating more fears and damage to society.

A lot of scholars see the media publicity of terrorism as very inappropriate. Media coverage of some terrorist acts is classified as ethically problematic and found to help terrorism or contribute to the prolongation of violent episodes. The 444-day detention of the American diplomats in Tehran (1979–1980) is a classic example of how terrorists used the media for their gain. The hostages were released only after their captors achieved maximum publicity from the media. The media placed President Jimmy Carter in a very difficult position when they repeatedly dwelled on the suffering of the hostages and their families, thereby exerting pressure on the president to take action in favour of the terrorists. [29]

The media also have ways to ensure that plans and strategies get to the terrorists ahead of their implementation. This is bad as the terrorists can change strategy to beat law enforcement and remain a step ahead of them. Having stated this, the media can also be used as a tactical strategy by the community and law enforcement to ward off attacks by overhyping the efforts of the community and others to discourage terrorist attacks. It is necessary, therefore, to avoid giving out information to the media that will jeopardize the safety of the community or the plans of law enforcement to protect the community.

Though it is also ethical to allow the media go about their duties without interruption, for the general benefit of humankind, where it concerns terrorism it is important to give the media certain restrictions that will help to reduce the fear of citizens. Of course, media restrictions will weaken the terrorists' strategy of using the media to attain popularity or as a medium to showcase their dastardly acts.

---

[29] Cohen-Almagor, R. (2005). Media coverage of acts of terrorism: Troubling episodes and suggested guidelines. *Canadian Journal of Communication,* ISSN: 1499-6642. Available at http://www.cjc-online.ca/index.php/journal/article/view/1579/1734.

Role of Women in Terrorism

In analysing the role of women in terrorism, it is important to point out the fact that women are involved at two ends. There are women involved in preventing terrorism just as they are involved in the acts of terrorism. For those involved in terrorist acts, they can assume the role as sympathizers, supporters, or major actors in various capacities. Studies show that women are attracted by the same motives as men are. They are sensitive to and motivated by economic benefits; religious or ideological beliefs; grief over sociopolitical conditions or the loss of loved ones in similar struggles; and perceived physical, political, or psychological humiliation.

The exact supportive roles women play in terrorism include planning, handling logistics, writing or translating publications beneficial to the insurgents, preparing false travel documents for terrorists on missions, and management of safe houses. As simple as these tasks seem, they are very vital to the accomplishment of every terrorist attack or operation and must be seen as crucial contributions to the success of these organizations.

The ones who participate in very active roles are those who fight within the ranks. They are involved as commanders, executioners, reconnaissance in advance of attacks, shooters, or suicide bombers.

Effectiveness of Female Terrorism

The rate of effectiveness of female terrorists, especially those carrying out the acts of terrorism, is very high. Since women are involved in every aspect of terrorist organizations—handling logistical support, planning and operations—and their involvement is underestimated by their appearances, culture, and societal viewpoint, the effects of their actions are usually grave and come as shocking, devastating surprises. Records show that most attacks carried out by female terrorists resulted in disturbing effects as a result of female concession.

Between 1985 and 2008, there was a decrease in casualty rates from attacks by men and an increase in rates from attacks by women. This implies that as the incidences of suicide terrorist attacks increase over the years, targets devise ways of preventing or reducing the attacks by male terrorists than by female terrorists. It can therefore be said that the higher efficiency of female suicide terrorists is as a result of the fact that women attract less suspicion, are more able to conceal explosives, and are subjected to less stringent security scrutiny than men as, at first glance, they do not fit the stereotype of terrorists.

The society where female terrorists operate also boosts their effectiveness by allowing the use of loose, full-body clothing which increases the prospects of carrying and concealing explosives while disguised as either pregnant or religious women. This is why Afghan, Iraqi, and Nigerian suicide terrorists continue to disguise themselves as women to penetrate target locations, just as the Chechen, Palestinian, Kurdish, and Tamil suicide bombers.

Another advantage for female terrorists is that the societies in which they operate consider vigorous searching and body contact as threats to a woman's honour, especially if she is Muslim. This means that explosives hidden in intimate parts of the body are less likely to be uncovered.

Terrorists have recognized the benefits of using female attackers for these reasons and because females attract more attention in the media when they carry out attacks of heavy magnitude. The case of a former child model Kim Hyun Hee, a terrorist who planted a bomb on a South Korean airliner in 1987, killing all 115 people aboard, is a typical example of the devastating effects of terrorists acts carried out by female terrorists.[30]

Motives for Terrorist Development

Two factors that may contribute to the development of terrorists are economic deterioration and individual causes. Terrorism may evolve from economic deterioration when, for example, a country's government neglects its people, as in cases of terrorism in the Niger Delta region of Nigeria, as the government has neglected this oil rich region. While the government sucked the region dry of its natural resources and destroyed its means of livelihood through environmental pollution, people lived in abject poverty, and the region was left out of the nation's development agenda, causing deterioration in their economic well-being. This, of course, led to the uprising that transformed into decades of terrorism, mildly referred to as "militancy", in the region.

Individual causes of terrorism arise from personal decisions that have been made based on various factors that influenced the terrorist. They may be motivated by ideological, national, religious, or even personal reasons or experiences. An example is the religious undertone the Boko Haran terrorist group has, including their ideology that Western education is bad for their religion.

The similarities on how these two factors contribute to the development of terrorism include the fact that they both have to do with personal experiences as motivational factors for the terrorist. Economic deterioration personally affects every individual in communities that have been neglected. This gives the individual, a prospective terrorist,

---

[30] Harmon, C. C., and Holmes-Eber, P. (2014). Women in terrorists undergrounds. *Global ECCO*. Available at https://globalecco.org/women-in-terrorist-undergrounds.

the push to have a personal reason to join a terrorist group and a sense of conviction for the reason behind his or her involvement. The same goes for prospective terrorists motivated by individual causes. They all have personal convictions based on ideologies, their religious beliefs, or personal experiences, such as attacks or violations, that motivate them to join terrorist groups.

For both factors, the economic and social statuses of individuals involved in terrorism is an element for motivation since their involvement promises to provide a better standard of living for them. The Almajiris of northern Nigeria are typical examples of this. Not all of them agree with the ideology of the Boko Haram sect or have personal experiences that push them into terrorism. Their state of abject poverty and the promises of a brighter future may be their major motivating factors.

The Niger Delta militants are examples as well. Though their agitation was ignited by economic deterioration, individually, each terrorists had a motive to enrich himself or herself and to live better a better life by participating in actions that involved kidnapping of oil workers for ransom and threatening the stability of state governments in the region to extort huge sums of money from their governors.

As seen by terrorists, there is also some form of importance or self-realization attached to being a terrorist. Through their affiliations, they become forces to be reckoned with. As most governments or organizations attempt to negotiate with terrorists, some sort of fame accompanies it. These terrorists never enjoyed anything of this sort in the past, so it may serve as a motivator for others to join terrorist groups. This applies to both motivational factors.

The differences are that terrorism caused by economic deterioration may not exist for long if a solution is rendered. Therefore, since the terrorists know their actions may end when a solution comes, they see this as a short-term way to enrich themselves, and the terrorists are ruthless with their actions in generating financial gratification. Once their peers see the new lifestyle of affluence being enjoyed, they get encouraged to join these groups. Terrorism from individual causes, however, lasts for a long time. The motivation comes from the long-lasting benefits received by the terrorists. This comes in the form of money, material possessions from looting and vandalizing areas of their attacks, as well as other benefits.

The benefits acts of terrorism against a government that allows economic deterioration bring for the terrorists is a good motivating factor. An example is the amnesty program for the Niger Delta terrorists in Nigeria. It witnessed great improvements in the social status of terrorists and their families in exchange for their weapons. This gesture multiplied the number of terrorists in the Niger Delta as every youth wanted a taste of the largesse. While economic deterioration causes terrorist groups to think in the direction of social change for their group, those motivated by individual causes think of self-benefits.

Based on this comparison, it appears that the benefits or the motivator for joining a terrorist group is more for personal benefits. The two factors discussed outline the fact that motivation by these categories of terrorists are mainly based on financial gains and status uplifting, not for the groups they are joining, but for themselves. In essence, most terrorists' motivations is self-based.

Gender Supremacy/Equality in Terrorist Organizations

Gender imbalance and superiority over women exist within terrorist organizations. When it comes to terrorist missions, both genders are seen as equal. But outside that, the female is inferior to the male terrorist. This implies that women do not have total control over their lives and can be manipulated or even instructed to take decisions against their own wills, and then carry out deadly operations as equals to their male counterparts.

In a lot of cases, abduction and coercion are reportedly used as a means of recruiting female terrorists. Most of them may carry out their actions as a result of fear or compulsion and are subjected to oppression by male terrorists. In Nigeria, most female suicide terrorists captured by Boko Haram are forced into such actions when terrorists hold back their family members and threaten to kill them for non-compliance. A clear case of this occurred on January 11, 2015, in Potiskum, north-east Nigeria. Two girls were forced into suicide terrorism and exploded in a crowded market, killing twenty people.[31]

In comparing these to other barriers that women face, such as domestic and sex slavery, the act of suicide bombing is more gruesome since there are no chances of surviving to remould a life. Domestic and sex slavery still provides an opportunity for victims to rebuild their lives, and in some cases, use their experiences to help prevent or reduce the impact of such actions in future.

The Element of Surprise

Since terrorists use the surprise strategy which, of course, adds to the psychological imbalance of victims, it is vital to plan ways to prevent or reduce the effect of terrorism when it occurs, seeing that it is imminent and owing to the increasing spate of insurgency across the world. While the military and law enforcement battle in the direct war against insurgents, it is important that communities adopt prevention and preparedness strategies to reduce the impact of these attacks on the population if or when they come. Community intelligence gathering and dissemination of useful information on intended terrorist attacks to authorities as a form of prevention, and preparing the population physically and psychologically for imminent attacks as a form of preparedness are critical.

Suspect Handling/Terrorist Interrogation

In interrogating suspects of terrorism, it is indeed important to exclude psychologists from participating in the process if the suspect's human rights are to be considered. Due to the thoughts and beliefs of psychologists, the interrogation processes may take a different turn, resulting in degrading a suspect. This is termed an abuse of the detainee's rights and classified as

---

[31] Premium Times (2015). Militants force a girl, 10, to become a suicide bomber in sickening market attack in Nigeria. *AFP and Network WritersNews Corp Australia.* Available at http://www.news.com.au/world/africa/militants-force-a-girl-10-to-become-a-suicide-bomber-in-sickening-market-attack-in-nigeria/news-story/2c0bd b90065c1dc2978b4880c84c88e1.

an unethical procedure in carrying out interrogations. Degradation is a psychologist-designed experience for detainees and introduces techniques of increasing fear and reducing the ego of a detainee during interrogation. These techniques are clearly seen as degrading and negate the conduct code of any mental health profession.

To further understand the practice of degradation in a psychologist's involvement in interrogation, it is important to look into the records of Dr John Leso, a counselling psychologist and an American Psychological Association member who was consulted for the interrogation of Mohammed al-Qahtani, whose interrogation was determined to have been extreme torture. Though it was not clear if Dr Leso attended every stage of the interrogation, records reveal that he was present during an ongoing interrogation that kept crossing the line into torture. For example, Dr Leso asked the interrogators to play cards in front of al-Qahtani during the session to determine whether the interrogation was progressing as planned. In the view of Dr Leso, if al-Qahtani was seeking the interrogators' attention, it would confirm they were on the right track. Dr Leso also requested that the detainee must be kept awake and placed in a swivel chair, moving him in different directions to disrupt his ability to focus his attention on a particular point. This was based on Dr Leso's belief that al-Qahtani was relying on a coping technique consisting of focusing at a single point on the wall. As such, a combination of dependence and disorientation was applied in this interrogation and was indeed degrading.[32]

In using such tactics, the detainee turns into a victim and loses his ego and psychological balance. He also may be engulfed by fear and want to avoid further torture by owning up to something he probably was not involved in. Not everyone accused of or arrested for terrorism is actually involved. But with this kind of treatment, psychologists may force the innocent to admitting guilt for what he knows nothing about. Even when the detainee is very involved in the act of terrorism, this inhumane treatment tends to draw attention and sympathy to him from the international community as well as human rights organizations. In

---

[32] Olson, B., Soldz, S., and Davis, M. (2008). The ethics of interrogation and the American Psychological Association: A critique of policy and process. *Philosophy, Ethics, and Humanities in Medicine. Biomed Central.* Available at http://www.peh-med.com/content/3/1/3.

the long run, this support may generate strong legal representation to free a dangerous terrorist.

Addressing the dilemma of releasing a dangerous terrorist as a result of pressure due to degrading treatment of detainees can be addressed by strictly adhering to the provision of psychologists with clear, firm, and unequivocal ethical guidelines. Also, as long as psychologists involved are registered members of psychological associations, their local associations should be made to share the responsibilities for adverse actions caused by psychologists in detention camps. These would invoke sanctions on such members and create the machinery for checking unethical conducts regarding terrorists' interrogations.

ASD and PTSD Risk Factor Analysis for Victims of Terrorism

ASD and PTSD are unavoidable in most post-terrorist attack situations which leave victims, witnesses, or survivors with scars. The extent of disorder may arise in the aftermath of the attack from the severity of the experience or the effect of the actual action. It is worthy of note that ASD and PTSD have slight differences in the extent of progression. While ASD is an acute case and is easily reversible with proper care, PTSD is a result of higher progression from ASD due to lack of proper care or certain underlying causes which aid its negative progression.

Acts of terrorism inflict trauma on its victims. Survivors and witnesses can also be victims if they are affected psychologically from the effects of terrorism and terrorist attacks. The fear can degenerate into a worse situation that presents with actions such as disassociation from people, avoidance of eye contact, staying indoors, and other indoor fear-induced activities such as drawing curtains, getting dogs, and locking gates to get some form of safety. Hyper-alertness is also associated with ASD and PTSD. After witnessing or surviving an attack, victims are usually overly alert of their environment and tend to watch out for security issues that do not even matter. Always seeing things through the trauma lens, everything appears to them like a serious security concern, and this affects them psychologically. This condition, however, occurs more in children.

Victims who are less privileged, with less resources, are also vulnerable to severe ASD and PTSD. Since they lack the necessary social support and finances to handle their therapy and even live a good social live after an attack, their conditions may naturally worsen. An example is a case of a homeless man who experiences an attack and has no home to go to for safety. He is prone to having intermittent visions of a reoccurrence of the incident due to his vulnerability. The victim also develops sleeping problems which can result in more severe medical conditions as sleep is vital to keeping humans healthy. Developing a medical condition that fights the natural ability to sleep worsens ASD and PTSD.

It may also cause very high stress levels which are normally not healthy and may lead to high blood pressure, that can lead to further complications such as kidney and heart diseases. Victims with terminal diseases and PTSD are in danger of death from various ailments as they witness a fall in their immune system functions. This situation opens a victim to various other complications that may lead to death. Underprivileged people are the most vulnerable in this circumstance as they may not have the resources to seek proper medical and psychological care.

Also, a prior history of trauma or mental dysfunction may be a trigger in cases of ASD and PTSD. Someone who is having a repeat episode of trauma may go into a state of permanent depression or may even become suicidal.

In a case where someone with a mental dysfunction is involved, it may degenerate into a more severe case of mental disorder that will make management of PTSD almost impossible. Of course, the cooperation of ASD and PTSD patients is very vital in their recovery processes. Having a patient who is mentally imbalanced will, therefore, worsen the road to recovery.

Why Victims May or May Not Develop ASD or PTSD

It is common for some survivors of terrorism to develop ASD and PTSD, but some do not. There are various reasons for this, such as the extent of involvement as a victim of a terrorist act, for example, as in a case where girls were kidnapped by terrorists. While some may be lucky to have eluded rape, probably as a result of their physical structures or unappealing natures, others may have been raped repeatedly. It is easier for those with less physical trauma to escape being affected by ASD and PTSD.

Brain activities can also contribute to this situation when the right side of the brain processes information but does not transfer this to the left side, which has the capability to store long-term memories. In a case like this, the victim tends to forget all the details of the trauma and easily move on with life.

Proper management of victims by crisis workers can also prevent ASD and PTSD. A timely intervention, proper understanding of the victims' unique cases, and the right counselling and follow-up regime help some victims to see the assault as a stepping stone to forge ahead. Others may not have the opportunity to get this sort of therapy, and that may result in becoming patients with ASD and PTSD. The bombing of the US Embassy in Kenya in 1998 is an example of this. Some died, while some lived with the trauma. Passive witnesses and those who did not lose loved ones and were not directly involved would not be prone to developing any stress disorder.

4 | Terrorism Emergency Preparedness

Terrorism Emergency Response and Its Challenges in Nigeria

Nigeria requires a highly effective and organized emergency response mechanism to meet the increasing demands in this sector. This results from the surge in the rate of emergencies resulting from insurgency as well as their effects. A lot of countries have taken advantage of experiences in other troubled nations to plan ways to prevent, intervene, and ensure the impacts of acts of terrorism are minimized. The Aum biochemical attacks by Aum Shinrikyo in Tokyo, first with Sarin poisoning at Matsumoto city in 1994 and then March 20, 1995, at a subway, was a signal for the United States to get prepared for biochemical terrorism attacks which took place almost immediately.

Unfortunately, many other nations did not think that terrorism would creep towards them when planning for other emergency responses, so they made no plans for such a time when their nations would be torn apart by terrorist acts. Nigeria is one such nation that assumed its military strength and years of autocratic rule were strong enough to discourage acts of terrorism. As such, the nation's defence and internal security was weak in terms of knowledge and expertise in handling terrorism. However, plans and organizations for response to other emergency situations were in place but some poorly planned. In the past, the Fire Service was the only emergency response organization in Nigeria and basically charged with the responsibility of putting out fires, protecting properties, and responding to disasters within communities. In 1999, a comprehensive approach to emergency response was considered.

Since then, the emergency response system of the country has undergone several developmental overhauls, resulting in the setting up of emergency response organizations with better organizational structures, improvement of emergency response personnel through training, increased funding of the sector, collaboration with foreign partners as well as relief organizations and countries on improvement of emergency management techniques, and curriculum development in emergency management education programs. It is important to note that development in this area is nowhere close to achieving its goals, and emergency response organizations and sector are heavily burdened with countless challenges, including lack of funding for emergency management programs due to corruption, marginalization, political factors, social factors, lack of proper training to address the peculiar problems in Nigeria, and lack of adequate manpower.

In Nigeria, some of the human-made disasters include acts of terrorism resulting in petroleum pipeline explosions leading to severe pollution of riverside communities by petroleum products. It also leads to massive destruction of aquatic agricultural produce, lives, and property. Terrorist attacks also lead to loss of lives and property, injuries, displacement, and psychological trauma. Internal crises between communities, tribes, political opponents, and religious oppositions are other causes of violence-induced human-made disasters and lead to the same devastating results on victims and communities.

The most common type of internal crisis in Nigeria is religious violence between Muslims and Christians. Violence between these two groups grew in the last decade, claiming the lives of over a thousand victims on both sides between 2009 and 2011. Most of the violence was recorded in Kaduna and Plateau states. Benue state joined the list of those affected by internal crisis since the attacks at Zaki-Biam in 2001. All these have continued to the present day because perpetrators of these violent acts are usually not prosecuted because of their high-powered political affiliations.

Global Concerns about Biochemical Weapons

The United States, as well as every other part of the world, faces threats from nuclear attacks. At the centre of these threats are countries like North Korea and Iran, with their active involvement in uranium-based weapons of mass destruction. Concerned nations as well as the United Nations have stepped in to enforce compliance with the policies that ensure countries do not engage in the production of biochemical weapons. Such enforcement was evident when UN member states invaded Iraq to enforce compliance with its policies.

Today, there are several more threats bordering on the same issues as allegations against North Korea and Iran. Forerunners in the production of biochemical weapons filter global security agencies, attracting stern concerns. The fear of the effects of the use of chemical weapons on the global community and the intervention of the United Nations are the reason for the withdrawal of some countries, like the United States, from the chemical weapons program for attack purposes.

Prospective Victims' Consideration

In support of the resolve to ensure minimal effect of these weapons, the prospective victims were taken into consideration. It was necessary to note that adequate provision should also be made for emergency workers as they, too, are prone to the same effects as the victims. Since these biochemical attacks cannot be completely prevented no matter how much effort is put in place to do so, ideas were short on how to succeed with post-attack procedures aimed at reducing the effect of such attacks on direct victims as well as emergency workers assigned to locations. The RAND Corporation made suggestions to ensure the safety of emergency workers based on the number of emergency workers to be involved in a crisis situation, their proximity, their availability for training aimed towards any future occurrence, the cost of regular periodic training, nationwide synchronization of training focuses, as well as the presumed extent of damage and the area the damage covers.

Based on these considerations, it would be easier to have various multiagency synchronized training programs spread across the country, all having the same focus, training module, and operational plan. However, with proper planning and strategy but with a bit of difficulty in the implementation, programs to undertake joint exercises that include a multiagency hazard-monitoring effort and utilizing scene control to improve cross-agency accountability can be formed.

Though bioterrorism is not a very popular form of terrorism, it is wise to get prepared well ahead of its future occurrences. Terrorists all over the world are devising more creative ways to unleash terror against their targets as seen in the 9-11 attack on the United States and various attacks in the Middle East. More sophisticated ways of terrorism are being sorted, and bioterrorism appears to have easier and undetectable ways of causing devastating damage to even a wider range of targets.

History shows that biochemical weapons usage dates back as far as anyone can remember. Poisons used in the assassination of humans have been in existence all along. Toxins as well as disease agents have also been used as weapons of warfare in the past centuries. This is enough for the United States and every other country to become well prepared to provide adequate measures to protect victims as well as emergency workers if or when such an attack occurs.

Further Preventive Measures

Supporting negotiations towards a draft protocol at the Biological Weapons Convention (BWC) to prevent the proliferation of biological weapons and enforcing decisions made by the United Nations is one another measure that can be taken to address the issue of biochemical weapons. Another measure is to educate the public on the possibilities of various mediums being used as agents of biochemical attacks, thereby creating a vigilant community with designated locations and officers to take immediate action, including the evacuation of suspected biochemical attack locations and preventing its spread in collaboration with emergency experts. Also, ensuring the report of any suspected biochemical outbreak, no matter how small it may seem, will help to prevent the spread of any silent biochemical attack. Continuous research on quick-acting antidotes to biochemical weapon attacks may be a good project to embark on as well. And since biochemical warfare is aimed at any country, they all stand at risk of being targets. It is important that every country has the right to hold research stockpiles of biochemical warfare agents.

UN Intervention

The UN General Assembly mandate providing the UN secretary general with powers to investigate alleged use of chemical and biological weapons made provisions to permit the dispatch of qualified experts to conduct investigations and report back to the General Secretariat or the UN Security Council. This model was outlined in the UN General Assembly under its resolution 42/37C in November 1988. Outside UN authority, countries at risk of such attacks must plan for the doomsday and determine the best they can manage the predicament.

The World's Greatest Threats

Research indicates that North Korea represents the greatest threat to the United States and the world. There are several reasons for this, from the country's involvement in an unauthorized and a widely criticized nuclear program to the release of nuclear weapons in the past to its relationships with enemies of the United States and other parts of the world. In 1987, North Korea was identified as being involved in the in-flight bombing that killed 115 passengers of Korean Air Flight 858. Despite North Korea's removal from the list of countries that sponsor terrorism in exchange for its pledge to end its nuclear program, it has continued prohibited activities. Records show that North Korea conducted nuclear tests in 2009 and 2013.

Iran is another region that must be seriously spotlighted regarding terrorist activities as nuclear weapons in their possession will have severe repercussions for American security and the security of its allies. Leaving Iran to forge ahead with its nuclear programs will encourage Iran's hostile foreign policy, leading to severe confrontations with the international community as Iran possesses conventional weapons capable of causing a devastating effect on the United States and allied troops stationed in the Middle East and parts of Europe.

Restrictions and Limitations

Official agreements have been made to restrict the scope and severity of nuclear threats posed by terrorists. UN Resolution 1540 has given nations specific limits to participation in nuclear activity in an effort to curb the danger of nuclear terrorism. The resolution establishes legally binding obligations on all UN member states to have and enforce appropriate and effective measures against the proliferation of nuclear, chemical, and biological weapons.

Fear of Transfer of Nuclear Materials

Recent concerns about the rebirth of nuclear power production, that may prompt the danger of nuclear proliferation, will surely increase chances of these weapons being stolen and diverted by terrorists. Though the chances of terrorists carrying out a nuclear explosion are far-flung, this may become a likely situation if terrorists successfully gain access to nuclear bomb materials.

Responsibility of a United Force

The major solution so far that has been implemented and appears to temporarily control the proliferation of weapons of mass destruction is the formation of a United Force by the United Nations. It is comprised of several powerful countries for the purpose of enforcing the restrictions and laws of the United Nations concerning nuclear weapons. The United Force must look beyond these known countries and begin the strict monitoring of their small allies to ensure that while all the attention is being focused on Iran and North Korea, smaller nations are not brewing nuclear weapons on their behalf.

Military Participation in Domestic Counterterrorism

The Posse Comitatus Act, signed into law by US president Rutherford B. Hayes in 1878, bars law enforcement officials from calling on the military to enforce law on American soil. However, it makes provisions for exceptions when there is a military threat to the lives of US citizens. It also allows troops not operating under federal command, such as each state's National Guard, to enforce the law if called to do so by governors. Therefore, going by these provisions, the military can be called on to tackle military threats on American soil, such as terrorists' attacks that involve the use of military tactics and weapons of mass destruction. Experts have suggested that the war against terrorism does not require the brute force of the military but, rather, the deployment of investigative skills. As such, militarizing the civil law enforcement with military-grade weaponry, along with their investigative skills and techniques, has been proposed as a better option than inviting the military to fight terrorism on domestic territory. Nigeria could take a cue from this.

First Responder's System Objectives

System objectives can successfully be established across agencies which have autonomy. This is because most of agencies already have similar goals set towards these objectives and can achieve them by implementing them in their own styles, ultimately to achieve success. Monitoring and evaluation can be achieved by setting up a universal agency to ensure that the result is achieved. Once all agencies subscribe to a universal auditing agency, it will be easy to achieve the same goals.

In such a case, the auditing firm must come up with a solution, such as forming a task force of representatives from all the agencies with rotational leadership. This exists with the Multinational Joint Task Force in West Africa, assigned to end the Boko Haram terror in the region.

To achieve the same objective, such as ending terrorism, it is desirable to have consistent objectives across agencies. Agencies cannot have different objectives and achieve a common goal of ending terrorism. If they must succeed, they must have a common goal. But they must find a way to harmonize their jobs to achieve this. In Nigeria, for example, the fight against terrorism is fought by all agencies. Immigration secures the borders and hands over any arrested terrorist either entering or fleeing the country to the right authorities. The army crushes insurgents, but if any are arrested, they do not interrogate them. An example of an agency that crafted its mission goals and system objectives is the Multinational Joint Task Force, as stated previously. The challenges they faced were with leadership and the location for the headquarters since the agency involved several nations. When it was agreed that the headquarters and leadership should be rotated, the problem was solved.

Administrative Challenges with Public Health Organizations

There might be a problem with a lack of cooperation between organizations involving public health, law enforcement, media, and public safety. Swift measures must be taken to bridge these gaps and create the best practices for emergency preparedness. Some best practices include financial boosting of community development centres to upgrade their capacities for planning and responding to biochemical attacks. In addition, extra funds should be set aside for national pharmaceutical stockpiling in case of a bioterrorism attack.

Focus Areas for Emergency Preparedness

The six focus areas concentrated on to ensure preparedness indicates effectiveness in the goal of public health organizations towards emergency preparedness. Emergency planning and readiness assessment, disease surveillance and epidemiology, laboratory capacity development, communicating health risks and disseminating information, communication and information technology, and education and workforce training are all focus points necessary to improve the healthcare system in preparation for a terrorist attack. Lack of communication and coordination is also a huge problem, but with these six focus areas, gaps will be closed, though it will require better implementation and delivery strategies. It is also important that emergency preparedness programs are included in community schools as an extracurricular activity to improve and increase the awareness and strength in times of actual crisis situations. Just as schools have the Red Cross and Boy Scouts, there should be societies for emergency preparedness and terrorism prevention. Schools are a very important facility to involve in training and expose to rescue operations.

Improvement of Agency Coordination in the United States

The level of agency coordination after the 2001 attack has certainly improved. The extent of its improvement, however, remains a subject for argument. Improvement in this case means a better approach to incidents of terrorist attacks and a more prepared multiagency approach than there was prior to the September 11, 2001, attack. Some obvious traces of improvement include the implementation of the Standardized Emergency Management System (SEMS), the National Incident Management System, as well as the embrace of the Incident Command System (ICS). As usual, political factors come in to play when various agencies are assigned to participate in general duties.

Nigeria can learn positive lessons from this and implement them since the rate of terrorist attacks in Nigeria far exceeds that of the United States.

The challenge, however, is that the problem will always lie at the crisis locations where every agency tend to be autonomous and want to carry out their activities without receiving instructions from other agencies, who they think are not authorized to instruct them. As long as they are not under one umbrella, coordination will be difficult as nobody can effectively be held accountable for an action or inaction. Blame will generally be thrown across agencies, and responders from the same agency may tend to support their own. It is most important to centralize operations for more effective delivery of duties during crisis situations. Each agency may act as a cabal for various reasons, which may include corruption and ego.

Considerations for Disaster Management

It is necessary to form a very efficient and formidable multiagency by applying strategies to run it. This must include formation of a board with a member from each agency and with rotational leadership. By doing this, the loyalty of each agency to the central body will be assured, and the functions will be synchronized and more effective. More involvement from the National Assembly should be seen in emergency preparations against terrorism in Nigeria. This will be a very welcome idea as all agencies will abide by the laws established by the Nigerian constitution. Once a law is passed describing the roles of the multiagency, it will strengthen the bond between them.

In light of these threats, other forms of checking and controlling countries involved in nuclear activity must be put in place. More severe sanctions must be applied and drastic measures taken to end the threats. North Korea and Iran seem to have so much strength and can decide to pull the plug on the world. Scientists should work very hard on a nuclear weapon suppressant and other things to nullify the effect of nuclear weapons and get agencies to corporate further in research and training to defeat terrorism completely. Administrative bottlenecks must be looked at critically to allow a better flow of command and control of the multiagency before and after terrorist attacks.

Nigeria's Emergency Structure and Vulnerability

In terms of terrorism emergencies, the major cause of Nigeria's vulnerability is its inability to incorporate risk-reduction procedures into national development plans and the country's high poverty level. Again, the low level of disaster education is another reason Nigeria is vulnerable to hazards. Domestic terrorism motivated by intense poverty, such as the type of terrorism displayed in the Niger Delta area leading to pipeline vandalism, and that which promotes the recruitment of hungry youths and minors in the north are other reasons for Nigeria's vulnerability.

Emergency Management Structure in Nigeria

In Nigeria, disaster management is described as, "coordination and integration of all activities necessary to build, sustain, and improve the capability to prepare for, protect against, respond to and recover from threatening or actual natural or human-induced disasters".[33] The Fire Service is recorded to have begun disaster management as far back as 1906 and was given the responsibility of battling fires, saving lives, protecting properties, and responding to disasters of all sorts. Between 1960 and 1970, the head of state and state governors supervised disaster management functions, and in 1976, the federal government created the National Emergency Relief Agency (NERA) as a result of a devastating drought that occurred between 1972 and 1973. Following the UN's International Decade for Natural Disaster Reduction, the federal government established an inter-ministerial organ for the reduction of natural disaster risks in 1990.

In 1993, the federal government promulgated Decree 119 to further stretch its responsibilities to cover all types of disasters, also making it an autonomous agency under the supervision of the Office of the President. Act 12 of 1999, later amended by Act 50 of 1999, witnessed the federal government's establishment of the National Emergency Management Agency (NEMA), with the responsibility to take over the management of all types of disasters. The National Disaster Management Framework (NDMF) was set up to provide a total approach to managing disasters, with combined input from various players, including the federal, state, and local governments, as well as civil society organizations (CSOs) and private sector organizations. The NDMF displays a shift from response and recovery to other areas of disaster management and provides a regulatory mechanism which ensures efficient and effective disaster management and defines the exact roles and responsibilities to be played by all stakeholders.

Emergency Management Organizations and First Responders

Though the military, paramilitary, CSOs, and law enforcement all play parts in emergency response in Nigeria, the very first responders at any disaster in Nigeria are the citizens who, on their own, carry out the bulk of the rescue job before authorized first responders arrive. While this has its shortcomings, it has been found to provide much-needed assistance to victims. Others who arrive on site before the government agencies

---

[33] National Disaster Management Framework (2010), p. 1.

are community institutions like community-based organizations (CBOs), faith-based organizations (FBOs), and non-governmental organizations (NGOs). The official first responders represent the federal, state, and local governments and are parts of official agencies. At the federal level, NEMA supervises management of disasters via its six zonal offices stretched across Nigeria. At the state level, the State Emergency Management Agencies (SEMA), and at the local government level, the Local Emergency Management Agencies (LEMA) see to the management of disasters in their various jurisdictions. They are also charged with the responsibilities of developing capabilities to prepare, prevent, respond to, and recover from disasters. These efforts are all complemented by emergency management volunteers (EMV).

Risk Assessment and Identification Agencies as Preventive Measures

As a form of emergency prevention, some federal institutions and agencies have been given the required technical skills to carry out risk assessment and identification. NEMA has established the Geographic Information System (GIS) unit in its Department of Planning, that is saddled with the responsibility of working on flood and landslide hazard maps for remote areas using techniques for wider assessments across the country. Its academic system ensures that six federal universities include GIS courses in their curricula and the skills required to develop their risk-mapping scheme.

The African Regional Centre for Space Technology and Education-English (ARCSSTE-E), affiliated with the United Nations, helps to develop skills for satellite communications applications, particularly for rural development and health services; distance education; disaster mitigation; navigation and regional networking with industries. ARCSSTE-E has successfully executed and is presently carrying out projects like monitoring deforestation and implications for biodiversity in Nigeria, the Nigerian mesoscale experiment (Desertification EPR and DRR National Capacity Assessment Nigeria, p. 17), impact modelling using field measurements from a distributed sensors network, climate impact modelling, impacts of global climate change in the African region, and so on.

The Nigerian Red Cross Society (NRCS) also supports the Federal Ministry of Health Integrated Disease Surveillance and Response system (IDSR) in Nigeria by providing local awareness of the hazards the communities are exposed to. The Red Cross assists vulnerable populations with the interpretation of early warning information and to adopt measures for taking appropriate and timely steps to minimize mortality and morbidity rates.

The emergency preparedness unit of Medecins Sans Frontieres (MSF; Doctors without Borders) has an active close-watch system that is harmonized with that of the Federal Ministry of Health's system. Data is obtained from all stakeholders in order to take immediate action. Their system allows local government workers to give early alerts any suspected or occurring epidemic.

In August 2008, the UN Development Program (UNDP) funded the establishment of the flood early warning system. Worried about the huge economic losses from nationwide floods and determined to create preventive moves towards the management of floods, the federal Ministry of Environment and the UNDP jointly organized the National Workshops on Flood Early Warning Systems (FEWS). This initiative is to create awareness and a means to establish and implement the system around the country. In collaboration with UNICEF and WHO, NEMA has conducted a vulnerability and capacity analysis (VCA) in twenty-one local government areas across the country. The goal is to conduct the VCA assessment exercise in all 774 local government areas of Nigeria. Civil society networks, such as the West Africa Civil Society network and the WANEP, are also involved in mapping vulnerabilities and act as supplementary early warning systems.

Existing Capacity at the State Level

Since there are thirty-six states in Nigeria with various risk assessment mechanisms, it may be difficult to put all the records in one piece. However, it is established that various state risk assessment organs work in collaboration with some of the previously mentioned agencies to prevent disasters. Some states and local governments also hire private hands as many local governments in Lagos state have resident engineers assigned to monitor the drainage and runoff situations. They report analytically to local government authorities to ensure appropriate and effective actions which serve as early warnings are taken.

Challenges in the Nigeria Emergency Management Sector

Numerous challenges face the emergency management systems in Nigeria. They include inadequate funding, differences in emergency management structures at the state level, inadequate disaster management education, lack of collaboration among different levels of government agencies, and corruption.

Inadequate Funding

Due to the amount of funds allocated by NEMA for risk reduction, the act of disaster risk reduction suffers inadequacies and cannot meet specific standards for risk management operations. This reduces the ability to execute recommended risk-reducing strategies as applies to various crisis situations. Inadequate funding is one of the reasons that out of the 774 existing local government areas in Nigeria, NEMA has employed VCAs in only twenty-one of them. Also, many disaster risk reduction publications produced in English by emergency management agencies are yet to be translated into local languages. These publications contain very important information as well as roles and responsibilities of citizens during a crisis situation. Therefore, they could do a lot of good and reduce the impacts of disasters if they were printed in local languages which enable the locals to read and understand them.

Differences in Emergency Management Structures at the State Level

Each of the thirty-six states in Nigeria is expected to have a SEMA. However, only twenty-two states have emergency management agencies backed by law. Others still hold on to the former ad hoc emergency management system run from the offices of state governors. It is very difficult to standardize procedures, coordinate resources, and collaborate when state agencies have different emergency management structures.

Inadequate Disaster Management Education

No institution in Nigeria ran independent courses in emergency management or risk reduction until very recently. Even with this, the curriculum is not rich enough to cover critical areas. Very few professionals from emergency agencies are sent abroad for training. Of those who do, on their return, there is no program set to pass knowledge down. As a result, knowledge is stuck with a few, though the work is enormous and requires more expertise. Furthermore, since tertiary institutions in Nigeria do not offer such courses, it limits the number of professionals who can be trained in emergency services. Most unfortunate also is the fact that the government does not give independent professionals the opportunities to contribute their knowledge and expertise to the development of this sector due to unknown reasons.

Lack of Multiagency Collaboration

Inadequate collaboration and cooperation among multiagencies and different levels of government, particularly the lower cadre, pose a challenge to Nigeria's emergency management system. This is a delicate problem that must be addressed because there is already insufficient capability to handle risk management in the country. Having problems with collaboration will further destroy the already weak emergency management system.

Corruption

Nigeria faces an epidemic called corruption. Public officers and legislators are known to divert public funds meant for important projects such as emergency management and security. Since the government gives the highest vote of funds to these two sectors, it creates a channel for massive looting of funds. The result of this is poor staffing and materials to confront emergency situations.

Unavailability of Emergency Response Personnel

In most cases, response personnel are scarce to find at disaster sites, probably as a result of poor communication facilities or simply due to unpreparedness of the agencies for emergencies. Nigeria has had a series of air and road transport disasters where the unavailability of response teams to site led to massive loss of lives which might have been saved. In most cases, when the emergency response team arrives, it is already too late to rescue.

Disaster Prevention Enforcement

Lack of enforcement means preventing disasters is a very crucial problem in Nigeria. This is also due to corruption in some cases and simply negligence in other cases. The University of Ibadan suffered a terrible flood disaster in 2011 as a result of negligence in construction supervision which would have detected breaches in some fundamental building guidelines. This led to the death of a large number of people and the destruction of property worth over N20 billion. Libraries, zoos, fish ponds, laboratories, and their research institute were washed away by the flood, destroying valuable equipment and killing animals. These could have been prevented by following standards and enforcing procedures laid down to prevent disaster.

Lack of Specialized Training

Still on the disaster at the University of Ibadan in 2011, it was discovered that the few rescue personnel who were present could not swim. They also did not have any idea how to rescue or what equipment to use in the rescue of drowning victims. The sight of people helplessly losing their lives in the presence of so-called rescue workers still lingers in the minds of witnesses.

Misplaced Priority

NEMA has a lot of work to do regarding prevention, intervention, and postintervention in the Nigerian emergency response system. They appear to be less interested in the prevention and intervention phases, instead concentrating their efforts on distributing relief material as post-intervention measures. Of course, the reasons are not far-fetched. As long as contracts are being placed by the agency for the acquisition of these essential materials for relief, it is obvious that officials are busy conducting their business of buying and selling these products rather than emergency response. Furthermore, in the past, crisis workers have been seen sharing relief materials amongst themselves and giving the leftovers to victims.

Assumption of Duties/Responsibilities

Obviously, NEMA's impact is limited due to staffing issues across the country. Unfortunately, paramilitary agencies like the Civil Defence Corps assume they are the Nigerian military or law enforcement. Rather than joining hands with NEMA to carry out rescue duties as contained in the Civil Defence Act, civil defence personnel are usually found loitering about disaster sites, claiming they are protecting the area from violence. This leaves the understaffed NEMA more devastated. Other agencies, such as the Army Engineers and the Fire Service, that can be of immense assistance in some specialized ways, are restricted to military duties and fire safety operations, respectively.

Political Interference

Nigeria is huge, and as such, the federal response agencies requires assistance from state and local government response agencies. Disaster management and response initiatives in most cases are completely absent at the local government level. This is because some local government administrative systems are not functional as a result of the undemocratic tendencies of state governors who disrespect section 7 of Nigeria's constitution, which ensures the institutionalization of democratic structures at the grassroots level. Local government officials can only put workable disaster management infrastructure and services in place when the local governments are democratically administered.

After Hurricane Katrina in New Orleans, Louisiana, all levels of government, from the local council to the federal level, participated in the rescue efforts. In all phases of emergency response to Hurricane Katrina in August 2005, it is evident that disaster management involves every citizen and government. The most critical action is for emergency response to be properly legislated, regulated, and enforced by government agencies at all levels.

Existing Opportunities

Since there are no challenges without opportunities to solve the problems, three opportunities have been identified. It is hoped that authorities will see these opportunities and take advantage of them to improve Nigeria's emergency management system.

1. *Addition of Emergency Management in School Curricula.* It is of the utmost importance that the federal government includes emergency management courses in higher education curricula. Currently, only six Nigerian universities have developed curricula in disaster risk reduction for bachelor's and master's degrees in disaster risk management. Since, with the support of the government, NEMA is responsible for providing a three-year funding for this program, NEMA should make efforts to extend this program to other universities within Nigeria.

2. *Sharing of Resources.* The Grassroots Emergency Management Volunteers Corps (GEVC) can be used by the federal government as a support agency to handle emergency responses. Since it was formed in 2008, the GEVC has steadily spread to over

twenty-three states, and it has a formidable presence in them regarding disaster response. The GEVC is not a government organization, and corruption found in government organizations are rare in organizations such as GEVC. As such, the government can fund GEVC to aid its spread to more states. These volunteers can become a stronger force in emergency response, with less challenges being faced by government organizations. Unemployed graduates with emergency response skills (which should be acquired through the one-year compulsory National Youth Service Corps scheme) can be hired as paid employees to engage in emergency response operations such as educating communities or taking part in the actual act as first responders. The viability and feasibility of this strategy can be checked and worked out between NEMA and the National Directorate for Employment.

3. *International Alliance.* Due to terrorist attacks carried out on international targets, such as the one on the UN headquarters in Abuja in 2011 by Boko Haram, Nigeria has become a nation getting much attention by the international community. This and other such attacks can enable an alliance between Nigeria and other nations to work towards fighting terrorism and mitigating the effects of terrorist attacks. Since emergency response is also designed to reduce the impact of such attacks, more training and equipment can be acquired for Nigerian first responders to help build the emergency response system in Nigeria. In protecting some of its economic interests, such as crude oil importation from Nigeria, US and other governments may be interested in giving full support.

Strategic Objectives of Emergency Response Agencies

Emergency response agencies are charged with various responsibilities which must have a universal goal. In whatever part of the world one finds himself or herself, an emergency is exactly the same. Though based on a couple factors, response strategies may differ in application. However, the goals of the responders remain the same. They include tracking and analysing risk and vulnerability, as well as integrating findings into humanitarian and development programming. Others are to support vulnerable populations to better cope with shocks by responding early to warning signals, by reducing post-crisis recovery times, and by building the capacity of national actors. It is also the goal of first responders to deliver coordinated and integrated life-saving assistance to people affected by emergencies.

Priority Actions

While pursuing these vital goals, it is important to prioritize actions as a first responder by improving access to protection and assistance to civilians in conflict areas, including the internally displaced. It is also mandatory to provide essential primary and secondary health services (preventive and curative) by addressing chronic diseases, reproductive health, infant and child health, and treatment and prevention of acute malnutrition. Responders also must increase monitoring of early warning signs and early detection of possible outbreaks of communicable diseases so as to initiate an effective response for disease control. Required and urgent intervention are needed where necessary to promote livelihoods, rehabilitate damaged infrastructures, and support income-generating activities to provide immediate economic relief to affected populations in rural and urban areas.

In assessing the performances of the response system in Nigeria, it is important to weigh the activities of the agencies involved in emergency response and measure their activities with the objectives and goals stated previously. Apart from having investigative and regulatory bodies, the emergency response system must have an auditing mechanism put in place. This will ensure that all response agencies are put in proper check.

Disaster Management and Nigeria's Development Policy

Disaster management is noted as a critical development concern in Nigeria. Though this is a recognized concern, it has not, in the recent past, been given sufficient priority in development planning and administration.

This may be based on the false assumption that Nigeria is not prone to disasters. This, however, is a baseless assumption and can easily be flawed, bearing in mind the frequency spate of public emergencies in Nigeria today. Based on their findings, recent researchers have written that Nigeria is characterized with high disaster vulnerability.

Nigeria has recorded very fatal consequences of emergencies in past and present times. This has posed fundamental threats to public safety and sustainability in the country. Strangely, these are still truly valid reasons why the nation should introduce development strategies into disaster management and harmonize it with its national security. This is evident as the needs policy of the Obasanjo administration and the 7-point agenda of the Yaradua government were void of any issues pertaining to emergency disaster management. The Jonathan's National Transformation Agenda program as well had no plan for developing the emergency response system in the country. This is evident by the needs documents which focused on the concern of public security and reforming the security sector to establish an early warning and response system that will detect conflicts but not disasters.

The *International Journal of Liberal Arts and Social Science* volume 2, number 1 (January, 2014) indicates that concerns of public safety or civil defence should be dedicated to disaster management. Unfortunately, the document misses out completely on issues concerning emergencies. Jonathan's National Transformation Agenda gave preference to only two critical security-specific concerns, the Niger Delta and Boko Haram insurgencies. The Nigerian Fourth Development Plan or Grand Strategy (Vision 20, 2020, 2010) also discussed the issue of disaster management. Other than its indistinct mention of social and environmental protection, where NEMA was faintly mentioned, the document fails to recognize the importance of disaster management. This relevant exclusion makes the document technically and practically deficient.

This deficiency must have been because the document's drafters believe that security and emergency response are not in any way related. The result of this action is evident also in the document outlining the country's millennium development goals (MDGs), which has been criticized for not including disaster-specific goals. This clearly shows how the issue of disaster management has been so abhorrently neglected in the Nigerian government's development agenda. Consequently, the importance of disaster management has not been properly prioritized in national development policy, planning, and administration.

Effects of Citizen Participation in Rescue Operations

Citizens play a very important role in emergency response in Nigeria since it has been a culture amongst the people to rush to any disaster and begin rescue operations before first responders arrive. In most cases, citizens help rush surviving victims to nearby hospitals, thereby saving lives as well. The only problem with this is that their lack of knowledge in emergency response may either put the citizens or the victims in more risk while attempting to help. Inadequate personal safety knowledge of how to handle bleeding victims may expose the citizens acting as emergency responders to viruses that can change their lives for the worse. The victim may also be handled in ways detrimental to his or her survival if the rescuer has no first aid training. This makes it a requirement for everyone in Nigeria to be given some sort of first aid and emergency response training.

The Place of Disaster Management in Nigeria's Security Strategy

Though recommendations have been made for the incorporation of disaster management in to the National Security Strategy (NSS), the draft NSS document (2011) unfortunately does not include the issue of emergency management in conceptualizing and framing Nigeria's national security. The document only views Nigeria's national security from the views of internal security and territorial defence. In effect, the document merely defines background and concerns of Nigeria's national security simply in terms of political violence, violent extremism, communal violence, the Niger Delta, maritime security, and transnational crime. It completely omits the concerns of public disasters.

This distorted conception of national security in favour of defence is seen to be based on the draft NSS document, drafted by the National Defence College (formerly the National War College), a leading military institution in Nigeria. Its consideration and philosophy of security are bound to reflect an conventional pro-military bias and standpoint. It is therefore important that the issue of disaster management be given its required priority in Nigeria's national security agenda. This would necessitate a drastic re-conceptualization of the NSS in order to contain and prioritize the concerns of disaster management.

Considerations for Disaster Management

It is of great importance that disaster management is given its deserved recognition and position in Nigeria's national development strategy. Disaster management is a critical development issue closely related to national security, and both affect each other in some way. Principles of proactive disaster management should therefore be included in various aspects of Nigeria's development policy.

To amend the errors created in developing the security system without including disaster management programs, Nigeria has to return to the drawing board. It is necessary to design and implement effective disaster management programs to ensure that at every level—from the local government to the federal level—effective disaster management and rescue infrastructure are put in place. Areas of emphasis include the industrial policy, ecological policy, urbanization policy, infrastructural development policy, insurance policy, public health policy, and rural development policy. This would help in mitigating emergencies in Nigeria.

NEMA officials should be strategic when developing disaster risk reduction programs. They should ensure that such programs not only reduce disaster risks but also address other problems, like environmental degradation, climate change, and poverty. By addressing more than one problem, a disaster risk reduction strategy stands a better chance of attracting federal, regional, or international funding.

It is also important for NEMA to continue to collaborate with other relevant stakeholders to improve their work force and relationship. Registration of NGOs, CSOs, FBOs, and CBOs interested in disaster risk reduction should be encouraged, and the resources—personnel, finance, time, expertise—of these organizations should be taken advantage of in reducing disaster risks.

The introduction of poverty alleviation and educational programs will be important in addressing some of the root causes of terrorism. Furthermore, training of special counterterrorism units drafted from the military and law enforcement by developed countries like the United States will be of great help in the fight against terrorist attacks. The federal government can also reduce vulnerability to hazards by not only integrating risk-reducing measures into national plans but also by educating the public on the importance of risk reduction.

There should also be a formidable collaboration between the federal government and the governments of developed countries with vast experience in emergency management. Such collaboration can focus on training Nigeria's law enforcement agencies and first responders on the relevant skills needed to prepare, prevent, mitigate, respond to, and recover from disasters. Once all these are achieved with genuine commitments, Nigeria's emergency response system will experience great improvement.

Emergency management in Nigeria is a relatively new concept. Unfortunately, improvements in this area have been met with challenges, including lack of collaboration among levels of government and lack of funding. Some of these challenges, especially the lack of funding, may be because disaster risk reduction is not a priority in Nigeria. The suggestions here will therefore create the enablement for a change in the emergency response scheme in Nigeria if considered and applied.

Role of First Responders in Terrorism Attacks

In preparing for this sort of attack, the first responders must train members of the community to be physically and psychologically ready for the attack. The first responders may not be able to carry out the responsibility alone and may need help from able volunteers in the community. It is therefore important for them to draw up a training and drill program that needs to be mastered in the community. It is also important to organize programs that will prepare citizens emotionally and mentally for the attack. Town hall meetings aimed at generally educating people must be established, as well as an outpatient clinic to identify and assist those likely to have mental disorders. Those with histories of mental disorder will also be assisted to help balance and prepare them ahead of the impending attack.

Training programs on security alert must also be given to members of the security team in the community in addition to working with law enforcement in the community. This is important in reducing the velocity of attacks or even preventing them completely. Training on security measures that can be put in place to check the migration of insurgents, such as an identification and background checks on new members of the community, must be carried out.

Relief Organizations, Intervention, and Post-Intervention Strategies for Terrorist Attacks

Normally, the official agency responsible for relief in Nigeria is NEMA. Along with the paramilitary, they visit crisis locations to clear up bodies, body parts, and to care for victims of terrorist attacks, while the military is on ground to contain any remnant terrorists who may be within the vicinity. However, in most cases, there are almost no survivors as the relief agency only arrives when the coast is completely clear. At times, this is hours after the last attack. This delay is out of fear for their own lives based on the poor compensation regime available in Nigeria for relief workers. Non-profit organizations are also found at crisis sites with crisis professionals and much-needed aid materials for victims and survivors.

It is important that communities train their own rescue workers to fill in the gaps before NEMA shows up. This way, many lives may be saved through prompt intervention and care. It is also necessary to identify with non-profit organizations in preparedness for any attack to ensure that relief materials and psychological care are available and properly given out as a follow-up to arrangements made prior to the attack. To ensure total safety as well, known community leaders must team up with law enforcement to screen and clear the community of any suspected terrorists.

Disaster Response Strategies and Skills

Various skills will be employed in preventing the attack from occurring, but it is necessary to work out plans for intervention and post-intervention for an event that cannot be prevented.

Prevention Strategy

Effective security networking will be the adopted strategy. All forms of security measures must be put in place to prevent fear caused by the migration of terrorists into the community. The community will organize a screening and identification operation. Since communities in Nigeria are quite small with the ability to capably manage the population, it is possible to have everyone in the community given an identification card, with data provided to all security agencies in the community in case of forgery. Security cameras should be installed, and a uniformed law enforcement presence must be established with community vigilante groups working in close cooperation.

Intervention Strategy

Effective first responder action will be adopted. It is important that an effective training program be conducted for first responders which must also include members of the community to ensure immediate response after attack. Regular emergency and rescue drills must be rehearsed. The legislature must assign adequate financial aid to provide for immediate relief and medical support to victims and survivors. Additional functional health centres should be established with focus on emergency support and rescue, as well as stress-induced mental dysfunction.

Post-Intervention

Psychological, social, and physical follow-up checks will be the strategy to restore hope and confidence. The extent to which the crisis is handled will determine the well-being of citizens and the level of confidence they will have for authorities. It is important that proper plans should first be made to minimize the impact of the attack through the prevention and intervention preparation plans. In which case, the little that will be left will be to identify those with impending or existing stress disorders and giving them proper care. The needs of victims and the community at large should also be catered to by looking into the causes and ways the terrorists succeeded in achieving the attack. This should be followed with working out plans to prevent it from another occurrence. Welfare packages should also be made available, especially to victims and families of victims in addition to building the confidence of the citizens through various means such as the organization of workshops and reinforcement of safety measures.

Ethical and Cultural Considerations

The only ethical consideration available will be allowing civilians to use weapons during crisis. Currently, this is completely illegal since weapons are authorized for use only by law enforcement. In this case, law enforcement may use civilians more for intelligence gathering rather than for combat with insurgents. This way, the ethical concern will be addressed, and civilians will know where to draw the line.

The only cultural concern is the handling of women after the crisis. Male and female physical contact is very highly discouraged in parts of Nigeria due to cultural and religious beliefs. As such, it is equally important to respect culture and religion by involving female rescue workers in the training from the onset to take care of such concerns. They will be strictly assigned to care for female victims and survivors. In cases where victims must be camped, it will also be necessary to isolate the women from the men.

Risk and Resilience Factors

Various factors will be responsible for risk and resilience regarding the threat being discussed. Identifying their impacts on the recovery of citizens in the threatened community is important in ensuring a minimum effect and proper preparedness regime.

Risk Factors

Bad roads and exit network: For easy escape from danger, existing bad roads and absence of alternate routes out of the community will impede the smooth escape of citizens in the event of an explosion. The tight roads may cause a stampede, leading to more casualties. The absence of multiple exits from the community would also ensure a perfect ambush in favour of the terrorists as the entire community would need to run towards the terrorists to attempt their escape.

Law enforcement character and location: Within most communities, there is no established law enforcement presence. In most cases, law enforcement form patrol teams that merely drive through communities. Based on past experiences, citizens do not rest their hopes on law enforcement as in most cases, they are seen running in the opposite direction and only return when they are sure it is safe for them. This, of course, will give the terrorists enough time to carry out their attacks and even ensure casualties are at a maximum as they do not have to hurry from the attack site.

Poor communication and response: The telecommunication system in Nigeria is epileptic and may not be available when most needed. Assigned emergency numbers for government assistance for citizens in distress are not exempt from the epileptic telecommunications service. This means that victims may be trapped with no help coming their way. And this may lead to loss of more lives due to the delayed emergency response.

Resilience Factors

Enlightenment and community participation: In the past, it would have been difficult to get the community involved in educational programs aimed at enlightening them on the potential fears. Communities are now open to working together as a team to learn and rehearse safety drills and other ways through which they can prevent and reduce the impact of an attack. This will surely help in preparing them and will ensure minimum conflict.

Psychological counselling: The minds of the members of the community should be well prepared through psychological education, assessments, and counselling. The availability of financial resources within the community will make it possible to engage private and government psychologists. This ensures that stress disorders before, during, and after any attack are well contained.

Basic Needs

The community must have all the basic needs, such as water, food, and shelter, as well as facilities that can be used to camp victims after an attack. Therefore, it must be well prepared to handle post-attack conditions. This will ensure the comfort and provision of basic amenities to victims and reduce psychological agony.

Strategies for Urban Communities

Prevention Strategy

Community watch, security, and intelligence gathering are parts of a strong terrorism prevention strategy that can be used in urban communities. This is because of the level of development found in such areas, as well as the ability of inhabitants to afford basic amenities that can be used to protect themselves against terrorist attacks. Some of these amenities include the narrowing of city-entering roads, installation of numerous speed bumps, installation of thousands of security cameras, and the installation of concrete medians between lanes or at entry points into business districts. In addition to these, it is very vital that employed security personnel are given adequate training and communication equipment to report any suspicious activities or persons within the area to authorities with an arranged partnership program consisting of private persons or organizations, law enforcement, and government. This is achievable in urban settlements in Nigeria as security and community development are mostly the responsibility of the populace.

People naturally feel safe when tight security measures are put in place with functional devices such as closed-circuit cameras, communication gadgets, and patrol vehicles, loaded with law enforcement personnel. Psychologically, they are at peace since an extra measure to get the community well protected from attacks has been put in place. Terrorists actually avoid such places in Nigeria since they can hardly achieve their goals there. From past records, the areas that suffer more hits from terrorists are unguarded urban areas or rural settlements. The presence of security measures and good intelligence networking will therefore provide them a form of psychological assurance as seen in the case of Ahmadu Bello University in Zaria, ensuring stricter security on campus and assuring students of their safety following numerous attacks in northern Nigeria.

Preparedness Strategy for Urban Settlements

In preparing the populace for any impending attack and to reduce the impact of the attack, emergency preparedness training is highly recommended. Most communities, especially urban settlements, are endowed with specialists of all sorts. In these communities, there are doctors, nurses, law enforcement, members of the Fire Service, and many more who are capable of handling tough situations if or when they arise. It is therefore important for these professionals, as well as emergency experts, to organize training programs to create an understanding and awareness of the risks of attacks, and the importance of planning ahead as a means of drastically reducing the effects.

Parents and schools should also teach their children emergency drills for explosions to increase their chances of survival. This must be done to make the children understand it is meant for their safety, not to scare them. This way, citizens are psychologically tuned to reducing the impact of attacks on them and their community in various ways, such as ensuring that hospitals are well equipped and citizens have good knowledge of safety procedures following attacks.

The community should also be equipped with crisis workers to ensure that psychological therapy is administered immediately to avoid any stress disorder. These give members of the community some form of hope that survival rates will be increased, and the impact of terrorism will be reduced, thus boosting and improving their confidence psychologically.

Safety of Emergency Workers

To ensure the safety of emergency workers, certain practical issues must be taken into consideration. They include the number of the emergency workers to be involved in a crisis situation, their proximity and availability for training towards any future occurrence, the cost of regular periodic training, nationwide synchronization of training focus, as well as the presumed extent of damage and the area the damage covers. The essence of this will be to have a synchronized system of delivery during crisis, when taking into consideration the steps towards gathering information and taking and implementing these decisions.

In determining the most yielding yet easy ways to tackle these unavoidable assumptions, it would be easier to have various training programs spread across the country synchronized, all with the same focus, training, and operational plans. Most of the considerations considered easier to implement are listed below. They have characteristics that can be used amongst the multiagency. They are easy to pass across and apply to an emergency situation as a preparation plan, without having to gather all agencies together. They can be prepared separately, and all workers will be seen to have the same focus, operational goals, and procedures while performing their duties at a crisis location.

1. As part of preparedness efforts, put in place a coordinated, multiagency plan for monitoring hazards.

2. Develop assessment methods, checklists, guidelines, and standards to assist in hazard-monitoring efforts among multiple agencies.
3. Develop personnel identification and credentialing systems better suited to major disaster response operations.
4. Develop minimum standards for safety and health training for all responders involved in disaster response operations.
5. Develop systems to provide timely information on responder injuries and exposures.
6. Identify and connect with experts in hazard assessment during preparedness planning.
7. Develop a common terminology for disaster safety and health issues and processes for use during response operations.

For considerations that may not be as easy to implement, the issues normally identified in operations with multiagency presence were considered. Normally, there is a system of hierarchy operating within each of these agencies. It will therefore be extremely difficult to work with all the considerations without some hitches. Furthermore, it will be almost impossible to be at the middle of a real live crisis situation and organize a training for emergency workers at the same time. The considerations below may be possible with proper planning and strategy, but they will surely be more difficult to implement.

1. Undertake joint exercises that include multiagency hazard-monitoring efforts.
2. Use scene control to improve cross-agency accountability.
3. During disaster planning, address issues concerning safety equipment and multiagency coordination of safety logistics.
4. Develop guidelines for estimating safety equipment requirements for disaster response operations.
5. Provide on-site training, but not as a substitute for pre-incident training.
6. Protect the mental health of the response workforce by managing critical incident stress.
7. Improve joint exercises and training by incorporating realistic safety and health issues.

Definitions

Combat engagement: A face-to-face hostile encounter with the use of arms against warring factions. Neither faction is involved in any form of negotiations. Rather, both sides engage themselves in physical and technological warfare.

Counterterrorism: Measures designed to combat or prevent terrorism.

Counterterrorist agencies: Organizations assigned the responsibility of combating terrorism. They comprise all components expected to deliver strategies and well-articulated execution in engaging terrorists.

Counterterrorism strategies: Tactics used in the attempt to bring an end to terrorism. These strategies are usually developed by professionals in various fields who are connected to the issue and work out modalities for practical ways to apply such ideas.

Disarmament, demobilization, and reintegration: A collection of post-conflict interventions focused on retrieving arms, neutralizing combatants, reintegrating genuine ex-combatants in to civilian life, and preventing a reoccurrence.

Niger Delta Amnesty Program: Set up by the government of Nigeria to manage ex-militants from the Niger Delta. Their focus was a disarmament, demobilization, and reintegration program established in August 2015 to end the violence by providing platforms for self-sustaining vocational training and education.

Terrorism: An act of violence resulting or likely to result in major economic loss with the purpose of intimidating a population or compelling a government or international organization to do or abstain from doing any act.

Terrorist: A person or group of people involved in the act of terrorism.

About the Author

Dr Bowei started a military career at the Nigerian Military School Zaria in 1981. Before his admission into the Nigerian Defence Academy with 40th Regular Combatant Course, he attended Airborne Course 2-88 (for military paratroopers) at the Nigerian Army School of Infantry, Jaji.

After his early exit from the military, Bowie obtained a Bachelor of Science degree in banking and finance, a Master of Science degree in business administration, and a Master of Public Administration degree. He also earned a Doctor of Philosophy degree in public policy and administration, specializing in terrorism mediation and peace.

He has attended professional courses in terrorism, counterterrorism, and emergency management in Leiden University, Netherlands, the Federal Emergency Management Agency, in the United States, and the ASSER Institute in conjunction with the International Institute for Counterterrorism in The Hague.

Bowie is a Fellow of the Institute of Strategic Management and a Fellow and Certified Management Consultant of the Institute of Management Consultants. He is also a member of the International Institute of Strategic Studies and the International Society for Traumatic Stress Studies.

Bowie works as a consultant for the International ArtsGames Committee (IAC) in Canada, a training consultant for retiring servicemen at the Nigerian Armed Forces Resettlement Centre Lagos, and lectures Terrorism, Counterterrorism and International Security at the University of Lagos, for the Institute of Security, Nigeria.

www.ingramcontent.com/pod-product-compliance
Lightning Source LLC
Chambersburg PA
CBHW031127250726
48655CB00002B/557